HOW TO BEAT INFLATION
BY USING IT

DONALD I. ROGERS

HOW TO BEAT

INFLATION BY

USING IT

Arlington House   New Rochelle, N.Y.

FIRST PRINTING, JULY 1970
SECOND PRINTING, NOVEMBER 1970

Library of Congress Catalog Card Number 77-82893

SBN 87000-081-0

MANUFACTURED IN THE UNITED STATES OF AMERICA

To My Brother, Norm,
And His Lovely Lil

—An honest man's the noblest work of God.
—Pope's *Essay on Man*

Contents

HOW TO BEAT INFLATION
BY USING IT

1. The Death of

Independence

On Wednesday, October 25, 1967, Eustace Lovering Hathaway sat on the side porch of his "three decker" home on a road just off Division Street in Taunton, Massachusetts and, lifting his head so that his bifocals would come into focus, addressed himself to that day's copy of the *New York Times*, delivered moments before, along with a copy of the *Providence Journal* and the *Boston Globe*, by the Murtagh boy on his way to school.

October's bright blue weather had made the air uncommonly dry and the pollen and dust affected Eus's sinuses, causing him to sniff considerably, but the high sun, bathing that southern verandah, felt good on his exposed face and hands, and warmed the aging bones beneath his fine gray worsted trousers from Jordan Marsh and the soft virgin wool sweater that Margaret had ordered from Gladding's for his birthday last July. At age eighty–seven he was having a love affair with the sun, which he suspected was common among all who grew old in the northern latitudes. His yearning for its brightness intensified with each passing day of the waning season, strengthened by the disagreeable realization that he and Margaret would be unable to go to Florida that winter. Not that their health wasn't good. After all, Margaret was only eighty. It was simply that they couldn't afford to make the trip or pay for a place, even in a lower–cost area north of Orlando.

Eus Hathaway, who had been considered "rich" by the poorer members of his family, and "well–to–do" by most people who knew him, was, at age eighty–seven, a borderline poverty case. He had lived too long, he reckoned. He didn't know how he could pay for his winter's oil *and* his property taxes, too.

If there was to be much snow in the coming winter, he didn't know how he could afford to have his drive-way and sidewalk cleaned, as required by city ordinance. Surely he couldn't do it himself. It was certain, also, that he couldn't afford the "nine dollars per storm for any snow more than four inches" that Joe Nestor wanted for cleaning it with his Jeep and plow.

He and Margaret had lived mighty carefully for several years, almost as carefully as when they had first been married, more than threescore years ago, but the rising cost of living that had dogged them for years had finally caught up with them and passed them.

Eustace sighed and wished it were time for his cigar. He checked his watch. An hour and a half to go.

He opened the *Times*, first to the weather page, normally third page from the last. This day, because there was a full–page Montsanto ad on page 94, the weather was on page 93. He checked the weather's highs and lows in Miami, Orlando, Jacksonville, Houston, Phoenix, Los Angeles, New York and Boston. He thought briefly of how it would be in Orlando and Phoenix, and then sought to open the paper to the split page so he could read the news summaries. Instead it opened to page 49.

"COST OF LIVING SOARS HERE," said the headline over a story by Richard E. Mooney. "A FAMILY'S NEEDS FOUND 50% HIGHER THAN IN 1959."

Eus folded the paper to the spread that covered eight full columns right across the top of the page. Here was confirmation . . . indeed, here was documentation . . . of what he had just been telling himself. He had outlived his time. America was only for the young—those who were still working, still on the way up that old ladder.

Eustace Lovering Hathaway knew all about the climb up the old ladder. He was, he mused, the original Horatio Alger kid, and he had done it all with plain hard work and not much luck—except, of course, the luck of landing Margaret for a wife and having her at his side all of these years.

He had been raised on a crop farm—forerunner of the truck farm—in southeastern Massachusetts, youngest of five children. His father had raised vegetables in the light, sandy soil and trucked them to distributors who wholesaled them to grocers throughout Rhode Island and eastern Massachusetts from Boston south to Fall River. The farm had four work horses, one cow, several pigs and chickens, and one carriage horse. It was not considered a real farm because it was simply not a dairy farm, and was as foreign to most men of the soil and land as the strange tobacco farms in Connecticut.

The six–grade one–room grammar school had furnished Eustace with all of the formal education he would have for his entire lifetime. He had completed all grades and had spent a year "seasoning" on his father's farm until he apprenticed himself to a butcher. Two years later he was declared to be a first–class journeyman butcher, and two years after that, he bought a part interest in his employer's meat market in Taunton.

Taunton was, and is, a mill town, with moderate but steady incomes, and the owner of the meat market had stocked grades of meat that appealed to moderate budgets. Taunton is also a county seat, and in those days it was also an important rail junction point. Young Eus reasoned that with the mill owners, the prosperous jurists and the hearty and higher–paid railroaders, there was an untapped market. He induced his partner to run a line of higher–grade meats, along with the more modestly priced cuts, to attract the higher–income families.

The experiment in merchandising proved successful, and before long the well–to–do were providing as much patronage as the good eaters among the mill families. There was one difference: the profit margin was greater for the higher–priced items.

Eus saved his percentage of the profit as a minority owner, and lived on his wages in a boarding house near the fire station. The fire company was a mixture of volunteers and "duty firemen" who were paid on a per diem basis to take turns sleeping at the fire house. Eus supplemented his income by being one of the sleep–in firemen. That income, too, went into savings.

It was about that time that, at a church meeting, he met Margaret, a beautiful and blooming country girl from Vermont who was doing clerical work in the bookkeeping department of a cotton mill. He escorted her to several church affairs, and three times that summer took her by train and trolley to Rocky Point Park in Providence for a Shore Dinner.

When Mr. Simmonds, the principle owner of the butcher shop, decided it was time to retire, Eustace had enough money put aside to do three things: buy out the majority interest in the store, ask Margaret to marry him, and make a down–payment on the three–decker house that had six-room tenements on each of the three floors.

As it turned out, the top-floor tenement was vacant at the time of their marriage, so they set up housekeeping there. The rent received from the ground-floor and second-floor tenements (to be known later as railroad flats) paid the taxes on the house and most of the upkeep and the interest on his mortgage, as well as providing a little bit to be put aside so he could pay off the mortgage one day and own the house in its entirety.

On the business front, Eustace eyed the advent of packaged and prepared food with a mixture of alarm, skepticism and conservative disdain. He could envision a downgrading in quality as an accompaniment to the convenience and accessibility of the packaged, tinned and semiprepared foods.

He had introduced the "class" trade to his market, and he was determined to remain a class operation. Boldly he undertook the renovation of his meat market; like an expectant father, he hovered over carpenters, plumbers, and that new marvel, the electrician, while the work was being done. Then he stocked the most expensive meats he could buy, and garnered a franchise for the highest-priced canned goods he could find, S. S. Pierce (pronounced "purse") of Boston. Mindful of the care his father had taken in growing vegetables, he personally contacted farmers in the peripheral areas to line up the delivery of absolutely fresh produce at premium prices.

Three times a week he was at the freight terminal in Providence to buy the best cuts of meat right out of the newfangled "reefer" cars, which, fair weather or foul, were surrounded by vast pools of water on both sides of the tracks from the melting ice.

His buying missions began at 5:00 A.M., which meant that he left Taunton at a time when many people were just settling into sound sleep. Originally he had gone by train and had his selected meats sent on to Taunton by train, but in time he bought one of the first real gasoline trucks in the area, and navigated himself and his superior meats over the rutted and dusty sand roads (in summertime) or ice–slicked and slushy highways of winter.

The market prospered. In time it was necessary to add clerks. Eus still insisted on doing his own buying, though it meant arising at 3:00 or 4:00 many mornings and working through a long day until closing time at 7:00 P.M. He also insisted on doing his own meat cutting and doing the selecting, himself, of the fruits and vege- tables to be offered for sale to his choice customers.

His customers increased and were loyal. Profits mounted, and since his schedule precluded much frivolity, so did his savings account.

He still maintained his twice–a–month sleep–in chores at the fire house (the money went into a special account for Margaret, to be transferred to an heir in case one should arrive one day), and it was there, one night, that the brigade chief convinced him he could do well by joining the state militia as a quartermaster. The militia, he told Eus, was urgently in need of some- one who knew about foods, especially meats, and there was awaiting the fine rank of sergeant for anyone who could qualify.

Thus it was that Eus joined the Massachusetts State Militia. Thus it was that he was mustered in '98, and spent nearly a year at a training camp and assembly point in South Carolina, charged with the responsibil- ity of foraging and supplying the food and meat for a varying population of transients bound for Tampa, Havana or Manila. He was not displeased at being in a war. Two of his older brothers had served with the Mas- sachusetts Infantry in the War Between the States.

Late in 1899 Eus resumed his life in Taunton and for many years it was a very good life. He worked hard, but he was, he felt, amply rewarded. His accounts testified to this fact.

Eus worked six days a week in his market, and on three of those days he was out of bed at 3:00 A.M. and stayed until the 7:00 P.M. closing time. Saturday nights the market was open until 9:00. On Sundays Eus updated his books and brought order to his accounts, making entries in the precise script he had learned at school.

There must have been many sunny Sundays when he yearned to leave his account books—in the spring when the herring were running in the river, filling the entire male population with a resurrected excitement after the winter's fasting; or later in the season when the excursion trains left for the Cape with loads of blazer-clad, straw-hatted men and bright women in summery lawns and voiles and gay hats.

For years he resisted the temptations of idleness, striving toward a fixed goal of financial independence. There would be time for fun and a full share of life's pleasures when the goal was won and the future secure. Margaret broke the monotony of work in two ways. First was her ability to make a feast of the Sunday dinner. She, not Eus, selected the ingredients from the market, and with them performed a weekly production at stove and table that Eus regarded as unsurpassed anywhere. Her other great contribution was to keep herself beautiful, informed, up to date, and exciting, and Eus returned from his arduous chores to a delightful and constantly delighting companion. She shared his dream.

Eustace and Margaret invested in another three-decker house, and paid cash for it. Three years later they bought another. They were now landlords to eight families, including the two in their own three–decker. Rental receipts piled up in their savings accounts.

One great disappointment darkened their lives. Margaret became pregnant but lost the baby in her sixth month, and the obstetrician, his opinion having been confirmed by two specialists, informed them that Margaret could have no more children. Eus indulged in his first extravagance. He bought Margaret a beautiful fire opal, surrounded by a dozen small diamonds, mounted on an exquisite platinum ring.

Eus returned to work with a renewed determination to make money.

When he finally sold his market to his chief clerk, Eus had the three tenement buildings, a substantial number of shares in a local savings and loan association, four splendid savings accounts and a portfolio of good–yielding, extremely solid corporate securities. He was, by most standards, a rich man.

He had no knowledge whatsoever of the fact that insidious forces were even then working against him. He had no warning, no inkling, that before many years had passed he would be poorer than when he and Margaret had started out, the victim of an invisible strangulating force called inflation.

He knew only that he had worked hard, much harder than most men, and he had made himself rich. His limited knowledge of economics had led him to believe that he would be financially secure for the remainder of his life.

This had been his happy, short–lived thought as he set about the business of enjoying an early retirement.

2. From Dream

to Nightmare

In retrospect, Eus Hathaway handled his life and career almost perfectly. He created in fact what is—or *was*—the dream of the ideal life, latent in the hearts of all middle–class Americans.

It remains the great American dream, though nowadays additional education is added to the disciplined schedule, and a closer allegiance with the corporate world may seem in order.

Eus, in his time, was a man who "made it." He worked hard and with unwavering constancy. He selected his goal; he analyzed it; he set a steadfast course toward it; he arrived on schedule. He and Margaret were still young enough, when he sold his business, to sit down in that vineyard of his own choosing and enjoy the bountiful harvest that his own labors had produced.

Among all men, he could hold his head high. Born in relative poverty, he had, in the finest Horatio Alger tradition, worked his way to the top, neither seeking nor accepting help from anyone. He had paid his way all the way and had provided well for his own retirement, security and creature comforts.

There was no reason to fear the future, he thought, as he tried to learn how to be idle. The first thing he and Margaret did was to take a long, relaxing cruise, down the East Coast to South America, through the straits, and up the West Coast to San Francisco. It was one of the subdreams he had permitted to intrude on his fantasies as he invested his long hours in his business.

And every winter, for several years, he and Margaret had fled the severe New England weather. They had spent sunny months in Florida, in Arizona and in Southern California. They never splurged. Invariably they sought out inexpensive but respectable lodgings, and their sole recreation was either sitting in the sun or playing an occasional game of shuffleboard. Invariably they drove, because they wanted their car with them.

Eus never succumbed to the real estate fever in Florida and remained rigidly aloof from the wild land speculations that went on around him when he and Margaret were wintering in the area of Orlando or Kissimmee.

They lived carefully. They bought good–quality clothes that looked smart, wore well and lasted. They traded their old car and bought a new one every two years, because Eus had determined that was most practical and efficient. They were fussy about the quality of their food because of their years of association with the industry, but they neither bought it nor ate it excessively. Eus liked four good cigars a day and one tot of premium–quality scotch before his dinner. Margaret smoked cigarettes at the rate of about three packs per week. No one could call them spendthrifts.

Despite all their precautions, it simply didn't work out.

Eus adjusted the bifocals again and addressed himself to the Mooney story in the *Times*.

"The cost of a *'moderate'* living for a New York area family of four was $10,195 last year—highest in the continental United States—the United States Bureau of Labor Statistics reported today," he read.

"This was more than half again as much as the last time such a computation was made eight years ago. This increase, too, was the biggest in the country."

Well, Eus thought, it isn't much different in Taunton. Maybe it's a few dollars a year higher in New York or New Jersey or southern Connecticut, but, by George! a man with half an eye could see that the struggle for mere existence was mighty tough right in Taunton where, according to the papers, there was darn near full employment.

Why, the cost of food alone was outrageous! He didn't see how some of those big families in town made it— families with seven, eight, nine kids, and the father working for wages in one of the electronic plants. They were pretty good wages, of course, but they didn't buy much because of the prices.

Eus read on: "The major costs that rose the most were housing and taxes." Ha! He didn't have to be told that!

"The four–person family in this area spent $5,970 to maintain a *'moderate'* existence . . . in 1959. The 1966 figure, $10,195, indicates an increase of 71 per cent. . . ."

It cost 71 per cent more to live in 1966 than it did in 1959. Right there was the reason that Eustace Hathaway, once well–to–do by any standards, was a poor man. Poor, indeed; he was broke!

He was too old to get a job, and physically incapable of doing any work if he could get one.

He had lived too long. So had Margaret. All of his years of toil and skimping and self–denial had gone for naught.

Inflation, some confounded thing he didn't even understand, had impoverished him. Vaguely he blamed the government, and obliquely he blamed the voters. They wanted too much for nothing, he figured, and it was costing the government more than it could afford, which was what had brought on the inflation and had wiped him out.

It made his blood boil to think that he, who had started with nothing, an inadequately educated boy from a forlorn and unprosperous farm, and had asked nothing of his country but the right to work hard and save his money, had been ruined in his old age because his country hadn't practiced the same prudence and Yankee thrift that he had.

He felt betrayed by the country whose uniform he had worn.

Eus remembered things about inflation. He remembered that prices were inflated in 1898–99 and that there was a bit of a depression in 1901 that somehow restored the economy to its normal levels. There was wartime inflation, of course, in 1917–19, but he didn't recall that the high prices then ruined any families or brought about unexpected poverty. Perhaps there had been such cases, but he didn't know about them. He had been in business, then, and he remembered distinctly that when prices went up, people bought less. They didn't *contribute* to the inflation, he recalled.

There was a brief skyrocketing of inflation in 1923, and a short burst in 1929 before the market crash.

Inflation, he believed, came and went. When it occurred the government was supposed to do something with money. Cut back on spending, or some such thing. That Herbert Hoover, now, he didn't do what you were supposed to do. Or maybe he did it too much. Something went wrong, and the depression resulted.

Thoughts of the depression made Eus bitter. He had

continued to prosper right through the depression by putting in long, hard hours, and by giving the public the highest quality he could provide, at the lowest possible price. He prospered at a slower pace, but mankind's worst depression never hurt him much, though mankind's peak prosperity had crushed and ruined him.

Where, he wondered, were the values to be found?

The trouble started, Eus recalled, during World War II when the federal government began to increase personal income taxes and at the same time imposed taxes on a great many consumer items and consumer services.

Those little "service" taxes on everything—the phone, gas, tires, transportation, jewelry, luggage, nonprescription drugs, and so on, ad infinitum—mounted in the course of a year. Maybe you didn't notice it if you were working and could do something about your income. But on the fixed income that Eus had arranged for himself, the added costs took heavy toll.

When the government started collecting income taxes on a pay–as–you–go basis, many working people said it was easier on them. But Eus, who had allowed dividends to accumulate during the year in one of his savings accounts so that he could meet his tax obligations, learned suddenly that he had to make quarterly payments, in advance. This meant that instead of paying the government from interest he had earned on his savings, he actually had to dip into the savings, to pay his taxes. This reduced his capital, and, of course, reduced his income.

It was unfair, and he said so to the tax collector, but the fellow said there was nothing he could do to change the law. Later, Eus transferred one account to a mutual savings bank that paid quarterly dividends, and by asking for an extension of time to make his quarterly payment against estimated income, he was able to collect the dividends and meet the government's demands.

Even then Eus figured it was unfair, for normally he would allow the dividends to accumulate for the full year in order to receive interest on the interest.

When he took the dividends for the first quarter, he lost interest on that money from April through December, nine months. He was receiving 4 per cent, so he figured he was losing 3 per cent on the money he took out and paid to the government in March. On the June payment he lost six months or 2 per cent, and on the September payment he gave up three months or 1 per cent.

"They're destroying capitalism," he told Margaret. "The great capital expenditures in America are financed by banks that use the accumulated savings of little people like us. If they take away our savings, they're taking away the capitalistic system."

Margaret said that she didn't understand such things. Eus told her never to mind, most people didn't, a profound statement that, had he but thought about it later, accounted for a great deal of the problem confronting the nation and its citizens.

For the truth is, most people don't understand inflation, or its several causes, or its complex cures.

Inflation can be halted, but in a democracy it would require the will of the majority to do so.

Inflation can be countered—and beaten—by the individual. This requires only a knowledge of the enemy and of the courses and routes it follows, plus the application of specific countermeasures in the conduct and planning of personal affairs.

A forearmed and wary person of ordinary, average means can live with inflation and surmount its ravages almost unscathed, by application of the proper countermeasures, much as a person can live near a malaria-infested swamp, unaffected by the sting of the female anopheles mosquito, if adequate precautions are observed.

Inasmuch as inflation affects every American, whether he works or not, and will, if unchecked, inhibit and spoil the retirement years of almost all breadwinners, it is unbelievable that so little is done either to curb the disease or to disseminate information on how to keep it in check or to immunize oneself against it.

It is remarkable that a government so concerned over so many things, for instance the incidence of lung disease among 10 per cent of the smokers, can so completely ignore a malady that besets every American family and will wreak increasing havoc as time passes.

Eustace Hathaway knew as little about the causes and spread of the disease of inflation as he did about the etiology of diabetes mellitis or leukemia, and he knew nothing about the cure. Occasional news stories like the one by Richard Mooney in the *Times* provided him with his only information on the subject—and it came too late for Eus, much too late to do any good.

Trouble started for Eus and Margaret Hathaway when rents were frozen at the same time that the cost of maintaining his rental properties began to mount, and taxes were increased. It substantially reduced his net rental income, the part of the income that he could keep for himself.

Eus was accustomed to keeping exact records, a deeply entrenched habit from his years in the market. In the next ten years Eus discovered, by checking back through his books, that his real estate taxes had exactly doubled—a 100 per cent increase—the cost of fuel oil for those apartments where he provided heat had risen 37 per cent; the cost of maintenance, including plumbing, electrical work, painting and carpentry, had increased 300 per cent.

Though he had never before dealt with a government

agency or bureau on a firsthand basis, he appeared before the rent control people, and after three sessions, and a six–month notice to his tenants, he was allowed to post a 5 per cent increase in his rents. He had sought 20 per cent.

Even before the rent increases took effect, Eus knew he couldn't afford to keep his houses; that they were costing him nearly as much as their yield. No matter how he assembled the figures, Eus was forced to conclude that his rentals were producing only half as much money as when he acquired the properties. Net income to himself from the rents had been reduced from $4,630 to $2,886, even with a 5 per cent boost to all tenants. At the same time, it was costing Eus and Margaret much more to live—or simply to exist—with each passing day. He figured the increase in living costs at about 50 per cent higher than when he retired.

Viewed another way, the $2,886 that he now received annually from the rents, purchased what $2,164 would have bought when he retired, and the $4,630 he originally received in net rentals, would have purchased the same amount of goods and services that $6,945 would now purchase.

It's interesting to observe the simple mathematics involved in the destruction of a "good" investment within a period of ten years—all due to inflation.

Eus owned three triple–decker houses, with six–room flats on each of the first two floors and five–room flats on the top floors. They were nearly identical, as are many such houses in the area.

He charged the same rental in all three—$60 per month for the third floor, $65 for the middle floor, $85 for the first floor. There were two furnaces in each house, one that heated the ground floor and top floor, and a smaller one that heated the second floor. Eus provided the heat for the ground-floor and top-floor

flats, and the occupant of the middle floor had to provide his own. In one of the triple–deckers, Eus lived on
the second floor.

His rentals were $210 per month each from the two
triple–deckers that he rented in their entirety, and $145
per month ($60 for the top floor and $85 for the ground
floor) from the house where he lived.

It was a condition of the rental agreement that for his
rather inexpensive rent of $85 per month, with heat
provided free, the occupant of the first floor would be
responsible for removal of snow from the driveway and
sidewalks, and in summer would keep the diminutive
lawn mowed and the hedge trimmed. There were rose
bushes, lilacs, peonies and other perennial plants
around each house, but they required little care.

Thus, here's the way the investment looked when Eus
retired:

Rentals (3 at $60, 2 at $65 and 3 at $85) $6,780

Fuel (6 flats)   900
Maintenance (paint, paper, plumbing, electric)   500
Real estate taxes, city   750
                                                                           $2,150

Total rent less total expenses: $6,780
                                                                          –2,150
Net income from properties $4,630

If Eus were to pay someone else for the rent of his
second-floor flat, it would be $65 per month or $780 per
year, so it might be considered that his *real* income
from the properties was $5,410 ($4,630 plus $780).
This is the way he appraised his investment ten years
later:

Rentals (3 at $67.80, 2 at $68.25 and 3 at $89.25) $7,119

Fuel (6 flats)..$1,233

Maintenance .... 1,500 *
Real estate taxes, city 1,500
                                                    $4,233
*Maintenance now includes snow removal and yard care.

Total rent less total expense: $7,119
                                                    −4,233
Net income from properties $2,886

If Eus were to consider the savings on his rent at
$68.25 per month or $819 annually, he might figure that
his *real* income from the properties was $3,705 ($2,886
plus $819).

In actuality, the net income from his properties
dropped $1,744 per year. That's more than $145 per
month lopped from his income.

Within another five years, Eus saw his net income
from the eight rentals drop to about $1,000 per year.

Since the houses represented an original investment
of $29,000 to him, he decided to unload the properties on
the simple premise that he could earn more merely by
putting the original investment in a savings bank.
Thrift institutions then were paying 4 per cent, which
on $29,000 would yield $1,160. Moreover, the value of
the three houses had increased to about $12,000 apiece,
or $36,000, and that amount of money in the bank, in-
stead of yielding $1,000, would produce $1,400.

When he retired, the $4,640 net income from his prop-
erties yielded 12½ per cent on his investment of $29,-
000.

When he sold them they were yielding about 3½ per

cent on his original investment of $29,000 or about 2¾ on the enhanced value of $36,000.

Upon his retirement, Eus had $30,000 in investments in securities that were yielding an average of 5 per cent, or $1,500 annually.

He had $40,000 in thrift accounts—some in a mutual savings bank and some in a savings and loan association. The interest paid was 3 per cent or an annual total of $1,200.

With the proceeds from his rentals at $4,630, his annual income was:

Investments in stocks	$1,500
Thrift accounts in banks	1,200
Net rent from properties	4,630
Total income	$7,330

Fifteen years later, just before he sold two of the three triple-decker homes, an appraisal of his assets showed that the market value of his common stocks had increased to $45,000 and that they were then yielding 6 per cent in dividends. His thrift accounts remained static, since he had allowed the interest payments and dividends to accumulate—but he was then receiving 4 per cent on these accounts.

Thus, when he decided to get rid of his real estate holdings, this was his income picture:

Investments in stocks	$2,700
Thrift accounts in banks	1,600
Net rent from properties	1,050
Total income	$5,350

When he sold two of the houses at $12,000 apiece, he
had to pay a 5 per cent brokerage fee, which yielded
him a net on the sale of $22,800. He added this to his
thrift accounts, giving him a total in savings of $62,800
on which he was receiving 4 per cent interest, or $2,512
annually.

He retained ownership of the house in which he and
Margaret occupied the second floor. This produced
rents of $67.80 per month for the third floor and $89.25
for the first floor. His expenses were: fuel for third and
first floors, $550 per year; real estate taxes, $600; maintenance, $500; total operating costs, $1,660. With total
rental income of $1,884.60, this gave him a net income
from the house of $234.60. That lacked just a little bit,
actually, in meeting the fuel bill for his second-floor
flat.

Thus he calculated that he lived in a cost–free home.
The maintenance charges for keeping the property in
shape, for removing snow accumulations and for maintaining the yard came out of operating costs and freed
him of that responsibility.

After selling the two houses, then, this was the status
of his income:

Investments in stocks (dividends)....................$2,700
Thrift accounts in banks............................ 2,512
Rental from home 234
                                                   ─────
                                                   $5,446

He had increased his income by $1,096—nearly $1,100!

For a period of two or three years, Eus figured he had
outsmarted inflation. With a small pension from the
government for his service in the Spanish–American
War, coupled with his Social Security benefits—the spe-

cial minimum because his self–employment took place before there was provision for it in the Social Security law—he and Margaret considered themselves quite affluent.

Then the cost of living began to climb.

The price of food mounted.

And of clothing.

And of fuel.

And of medical–dental care.

The depreciation on his car doubled. The cost of a new replacement tripled.

The state sales tax was increased.

The town real estate taxes were boosted.

Each year, in order to pay his income tax, he had to dip into capital. Thus each year his income dropped just a little bit.

Then Eus was ordered to the hospital for a prostate operation. It was followed by a dangerous, costly and lengthy siege of pneumonia. Miracle drugs and an iron constitution pulled him through, but he owed a whopping bill to Deaconess Hospital, requiring a further dip into capital.

The worry over his condition caught up with Margaret and he had hardly begun his convalescence at home when a murmur of the heart developed into painful angina, and she, too, entered the hospital. It became necessary for Eus to hire someone to attend him in his own convalescence—first a registered nurse, then a practical nurse. When Margaret returned home, both the registered nurse and the practical nurse were required.

Eus made repeated forays into his capital.

His income from the capital earnings continued to decline as the cost of living continued to climb.

The two chartlines of his personal financial picture were on a crash course, en route to head-on collision.

It was only a matter of two years before the Eustace L. Hathaway family's "outgo" exceeded its "income."

Finally, "rich" Uncle Eus and Aunt Margaret, whose status had once been the envy of all who knew them well, had to appeal to members of their family for help. Most family members of their own generation had died, and upon looking around they found that most of the next generation were also retired and in similar straits, or living so close to the cutting edge of poverty that they were unable to help.

Thus, after a family council, members of the clan two generations removed were asked to pool their sparse contributions to care for Margaret and Eus, the survivors of a generation that had been all but wiped out by inflation.

Another session of pneumonia the following winter was too much for Eus. He died in his sleep, mercifully released from the financial worries he had worked so hard and for so long to avoid.

Margaret insisted that she would be all right living alone. The problem that she presented to members of the family was solved when she suffered a stroke that left her paralyzed but otherwise hale. She was placed in a nursing home where she could have round–the–clock care and ready access to medical help when needed.

The cost was prohibitive. She summoned another family council.

Margaret faced her situation decisively. She knew that there would be a relentless erosion of the few assets remaining to her. She turned over all of her possessions, including the remaining funds in the savings accounts and the unsold securities, to the state treasurer, and the people of the commonwealth of Massachusetts assumed responsibility for her for the balance of her days. She became, in effect if not in fact, a welfare case, a charity patient.

For the first time she was glad that Eus had preceded her in death so that he did not have to live to see the woman he had loved so devotedly and who had been his wife and constant companion for nearly sixty-five years, become a charity case in her withering days, a ward of the state where she had brought happiness to a home for more than fourscore years.

Eus's unswerving love for Margaret had goaded him to supreme effort so that he had accumulated wealth greatly in excess of the normal accumulations of his time.

The money alone was not enough.

He knew how to fight poverty.

He never learned how to fight inflation, and that failure ruined him and caused him to leave as a penniless widow, the wife he had hoped to surround with luxury.

The tragic fate of Eustace and Margaret Hathaway will be repeated ten thousand times over by those who fail to recognize inflation as the greatest economic enemy of modern man, and fail to learn how to defeat it and to bring it to terms.

3. It Ain't Cracker Jack, Buddy

That fine old American institution, Cracker Jack, whose red, white and blue box with the sailor boy on the front attended more ball games and movies than any other product of the packaging machine, had a slogan that was, in most opinions, uncommonly accurate: "The More You Eat, The More You Want."

It was true, to a degree. One box of Cracker Jack never seemed to be enough for a whole movie, certainly not for a double feature. If a lad were equipped with sufficient nickels, however, he could reach a point where he didn't want another single morsel of Cracker Jack, whether it was after three boxes or four or a dozen. The point ultimately was reached.

The trouble with government services, and one of the real causes of inflation, is simply that there is no point of satiety among the clamoring voters. There is no time when the people say they have been gratified beyond desire; there is no degree of repletion. The more government service they get, the more they want—and unlike Cracker Jack, it doesn't fill the recipient to the point of glut. Quite the contrary: one government service has the common habit of engendering yet another government service, like bacteria splitting and forming, splitting and forming, ad infinitum.

Even the most beneficial bacteria become harmful when they increase so rapidly and to such an extent that they create an imbalance in the economy of nature. Inflation is the malefic malady resulting from a superabundance of government services. Inflation of the kind that bedeviled the life of Eustace Hathaway is really as simple as that—it created an imbalance in the economy of the nation.

There is nothing very mysterious about inflation's cause.

There can be little mystery about its effect, either.

Lewis Carroll's Red Queen in *Alice Through the Looking-Glass* nailed down the apparent effects of inflation very nicely when she said: "Now, *here*, you see, it takes all the running you can do, to keep in the same place. If you want to get somewhere else, you must run at least twice as fast as that!"

The sad fact of inflation is that it's not a simple matter of merely running twice as fast—not if you're already doing "all the running you can do."

With Cracker Jack, if you eat twice as fast, you eat twice as much, and you fill up in half the time.

With government spending, if you spend twice as much, you create twice as much more need for government spending, and it isn't long before you're losing ground by doing "all the running you can do."

It has taken you just about two minutes to read to this point on this page since you started this chapter. During that two minutes the federal government has spent $664,000.

It spends $332,000 every minute.

That does not count the spending by your state, your county, your town, all engaged in providing you with "government services."

The trouble with the federal government's spending program is that in those two minutes it went $76,000 deeper into debt.

It was spending money it didn't own.

During those two minutes it took *all* of the annual taxes of fifty–four average American families to pay just the *interest* on the debt the government already owes. Just the interest, not a penny on the principal.

In a democracy the government supposedly responds to the demands of the people. Ideally, though, a government that exercises proper leadership qualities will warn the people when their demands are harmful, or when the unrecognized effects of their demands can cause harm.

To use a not too farfetched example, residents of a certain area, finding themselves plagued by mosquitoes, might petition the government to spray insecticide over the area. The spray would certainly kill the mosquitoes and would end the complaints of the beleaguered citizens. An unwise government or an ineptly led government might go ahead, without investigation, and order the spraying done. A government endowed with higher leadership qualities might first investigate the results of such spraying and learn that spraying such an insecticide not only would kill mosquitoes, but would kill or drive off the bees, and would sicken or drive off the birds. Further investigation might disclose that without the birds and bees, the trees and lesser foliage would fail to be pollinated properly and would die, or lose their density. And then deeper inquiry would reveal that without the trees and foliage, the watershed would fail to retain its moisture. This would mean that a quick runoff of rain or melting snow would cause flooding, and that the reservoirs of the area would not receive a year–round steady flow and seepage of fresh water to replace that which was used or was evaporated or was drained off.

A well–led government then would say to the mosquito–plagued people, "We would like to provide you with the government service of spraying your area, but it would be bad for you. It would cause dreadful spring floods and it would result in a bad summer drought, when you would be without water in your reservoirs."

Since we are pretending that this is an ideal government, one that is well led and responsible to the people, it would be nice to pretend also that the people would be responsible to themselves, and would say, "Okay, let's skip the spraying, and bear with the mosquitoes until we can come up with some other means for eliminating the pests. Maybe we'll try to attract a great many Purple Martins to eat them up."

It is possible that such would have been the response in older days.

It is predictable, however, that today the leaders of groups of militants would get together to challenge the veracity of the government's position.

"They are reactionaries," the militants would cry.

"They would rather see our people endangered by malaria than to spend the paltry few millions needed to spray in our area," the opposition would declare.

"A predictable reduction in the computable hymenopterous insects in a given area in any one season need not necessarily be reflected in the conveyance of the pollen from the anther to the stigma of many types of racemes, particularly the laciniose," would be the comment of a biologist at a nearby college whose wife suffers fiercely from her allergy to mosquito bites.

"The administration is inhuman and unfeeling," would be the opinion of a leading clubwoman.

The people would be aroused, and they would DE-
MAND their spray.

The government officials, painfully aware of the
functions of the voting booth, would spray, and then
await the painful results.

That's the way it would happen in the world of make–
believe.

In the hardheaded, practical world of modern politics, it doesn't work that way.

Anyone who has spent more than five minutes study-
ing the art of American politics—or British or French
or Canadian or Mexican or West German—knows that
the worst thing you can do is to say no to the constitu-
ents, to tell the voters they can't have something that
they have decided they want.

So the simple procedure is to abdicate the responsibility of leadership, to forget the obligation of the domi-
nant over the dominated, and to take exactly the
opposite tack.

In today's political programming, the procedure is to
maintain local party representatives who are on the
alert to all unmet needs that have budding recognition
among the voters.

Hence today, having been apprised of local concern
over the mosquito menace, the smart politician sends
research teams to that area to report back on the de-
plorable mosquito nuisance. They act under a special
supplemental appropriation of taxpayers' money garnered from all quarters of the Republic. Then, when
the report is ready, local leaders of the party are alerted
to the fact that the administration is willing to spend
some money for spraying.

The local politicians launch a campaign for insecticide. They accuse their predecessors in office, the
"outs," of having neglected their duty in handling the
mosquito menace. The appeal is issued to the central

government: please send us money for a massive spraying project.

At this juncture the top–level politicians get into the act—and "act" it is, rehearsed, preconsidered, well thought out. They talk and talk, and build up suspense, and finally make promises. And then, finally, the money is forthcoming, the spray is purchased, and the project is launched. If flags fly and bands play, so much the better.

In private councils, the professional politicians meet, and they plan for the eventual floods and the eventual dry reservoirs. They assign chosen members of their ranks to lead the people in demanding flood control projects and the creation of vast new watersheds. This dedication of new land to watersheds can mollify the conservationists who have been screaming bloody murder about the willful destruction of Nature's delicate balance.

Thus, one little government service has the potential for becoming four, five or a half–dozen additional government services.

It's good, old–fashioned simple vote–buying, but it's disguised these days under such masquerades as Regional Planning, Rivers and Harbors Development, the Corps of Engineers, and so on.

With anything but conclusive evidence, the federal government, meaning the administration and both houses of Congress, moved boldly into the field of public health and demanded that every package of cigarettes bear the admonition: "Caution: Cigarette Smoking May Be Hazardous To Your Health."

Yet with mountains of evidence on all sides, no cabinet member, no member of Congress, and not many politicians at the local level warn that further government spending may be hazardous to your very existence!

Tens of thousands of people like Eustace Hathaway have been reduced to poverty in the 1960s alone, and hundreds of thousands face the same fate in the 1970s.

There can be no doubt that this will happen. It has been made inevitable by government policies—government policies based on the demands of the voters.

What is the greater crime in a democracy—callous indifference or boobish naïveté?

When the politicians meet and deliberately and connivingly plan to spend the country into inflation in order to insure their political careers, do they, with a sin of commission, bear greater guilt than the clamoring voters who demand the services from government and who, committing the sin of omission, fail to comprehend what the ultimate cost will be?

The politicians were not alone in stealing the accumulated security from Eus Hathaway. His friends, his neighbors, all of the "little people," and all of his fellow middle–income Americans who were demanding more and more from government were right up in the front ranks with the politicians, plundering his savings.

For the truth is, government spending increases with each passing year; it virtually leaps with each succeeding administration. Those who are passive about it are just as guilty as those who foolishly clamor for it.

In the three years from July 1, 1964, to June 30, 1967, spending by the federal government increased by 33 per cent. The spending rate far outreached the revenue received from taxes.

When the politicians blamed it on the Vietnam war, they failed to comment on the fact that nondefense spending was increased by 36 per cent during that period. Remember, not all defense spending goes to the Vietnam war, either.

The government in 1967 spent $20 billion more than it took in.

In 1967 and in 1968, as a result of that government spending, the cost of living for every American jumped more than twice as fast and more than twice as much as the average annual rise of the previous five years.

Every American with a fixed income took a grievous pay cut as a result.

The poor people, in whose behalf much of the spending was done, had to spend much more for food, clothing, shelter, transportation, medical treatment, dental treatment, drugs, education and recreation.

Can anyone honestly say the poor were helped?

If not—who *was* helped by all this spending?

If the spending rate that existed at the time this book was written in late 1969 and early 1970 should continue unchecked, America will have a federal budget of $200 billion by fiscal 1970, exactly double the level of 1962.

This will move the general overall cost of living higher by about 20 per cent.

Does anyone want to ask the Red Queen how much faster we'll have to run just to stay in the same place?

Ask her, also, how you go about running faster when you're already running as fast as you can go?

Quo vadis, O America; *quo vadis?*

Whither are we going in America? Well, ask the dedicated spenders what's next on the agenda and they'll snap back with a ready answer:

Upcoming is the guaranteed annual income.

Utopia, paid for by Uncle Sam.

But who pays Uncle Sam?

You do.

Can you afford this new government service?

4. *What Kind of Future Do You Want?*

Eustace Hathaway would have had a happy and secure old age—and so would his wife, Margaret—if he had known about personal money management aimed at protecting his income and assets against inflation, and how to make profitable use of inflation.

It is the purpose of this book to assist you and guide you in learning the techniques of self–protection.

Eus Hathaway actually mastered only half the required technique. He didn't learn how to defend and keep it.

He learned how to make money, without help from any outside interests such as government.

He didn't learn what to do with it after he had earned it.

The latter is just as important as the former. It's why so many high–income earners in the arts, theatre, literary world and the like, find it prudent to hire a business manager to handle their affairs. They recognize their lack of training in the field of "protection" of money.

It's not likely you'll hire much expert advice to do your inflation fighting for you, so you'll have to learn all of the tricks of the trade yourself.

As a self–help book, aimed solely at warding off the evil *effects* of inflation, it is not intended that the reader be required to spend too much time analyzing inflation or the policies, both of government and of business, that cause it.

However, you will need a little perspective on the subject. You will need to know why we have inflation, and why it doesn't seem likely that it will cease to plague us for at least the next half–century.

Facing facts frankly, there is little you, as an individual, can do about curbing inflation or controlling it as an economic force. It's really out of your hands, and will be until there is a massive outcry from the majority of voters, and that, at this point in history, seems unlikely.

You have to know what causes inflation, however, if you are to gauge the degree with which you conduct your personal fight against it in managing your own inflation–thwarting affairs. You have to be able to spot the things that government does or that business does as either inflationary or deflationary, and to govern your own affairs accordingly.

This is the step beyond earning your money.

This book is a primer in what you do with your money after you have received it.

In no way will the information and guidance in these chapters help you in making your money earn more money, except as it applies to inflation–proof investments. Be mindful, though, that if you use your money in a way that takes advantage of inflation while increasing the value of your money, you'll be way ahead of the game.

Let's refresh our memories, then, on how—and why

—we got embroiled in this mess of inflation and how—
and why—we seem to be mired in it to such a degree
that we cannot extricate our national economy from its
eroding effects.

There would be something wrong with a government
if it didn't plan for the future. There would be little
value to the academic world if it didn't have strong
recommendations to contribute to that planning. It was
in the groves of academe that inflation got its start and
whence it was strongly nourished. Lord Maynard
Keynes, British academician and theoretician, fa-
thered the "pump priming" theory for creating "prosperity." Wearers of grayer or shinier heads will recall
that he entered the scene during the first term of
Franklin D. Roosevelt.

By the time the nation began to prepare for World
War II in 1940, the pump–priming theory had been practiced for six full years, and federal expenditures had
increased from $4.6 billion in 1932 to $18.8 billion in
1939. The unemployed, who were the intended beneficiaries of the priming of the pump with dollars, hadn't
been helped much—at least statistically.

There were almost as many unemployed in 1939 as
there were in 1933 at the outset of the federal spending
programs, which were predicated on the Keynesian
theory.

During that six–year period, Mr. Roosevelt and Congress had spent $59,736,533,485, most of it for projects
calculated to relieve unemployment.

During that time, because of heavy government expenditures and increased government debt, the cost of
living rose rapidly!

Those who were fortunate enough to be employed,
found their earnings bought much less than they did
before the special programs were initiated by the government.

No one complained much. Inflation wasn't a serious factor, not as serious as the army of unemployed, for instance, or the armies of Hitler in Europe.

After the National Guard had been mobilized and the draft law had been made operative, unemployment eased substantially, and as defense contracts were awarded to the industrial companies around the country the problem of idleness all but disappeared.

No one paid much attention to the old pump–priming programs. Some of them, such as those concerning agriculture, simply kept priming away, solving no problems and keeping prices high.

Not until late 1940 did the subject of inflation command much consideration. Then an editorial or two appeared. Minority Leader of the House Joseph W. Martin grumbled about it a bit, as some do to this day.

With Pearl Harbor, all economic problems were shelved for the duration of the war. Quite properly, nothing equalled the importance of stopping the Axis powers. The specter of inflation disappeared when wartime wage and price controls were imposed. It disappeared in the manner that the cells of cancer will burrow deep into the marrow and grow and thrive, while leaving the visible flesh, as seen by the world, as wholesome–looking and radiant as ever.

By that time, two forms of inflation, rather than one, were at work, both hidden from view by the shelter of wage and price controls.

Although the prewar inflation was caused by unbalancing the federal budget and increasing the federal debt, making money most costly to borrow and pay interest on, the wartime inflation was of the "classic" variety. It resulted simply from too much money seeking a diminishing supply of goods and services. With not enough of anything to go around, people bid up the prices.

When the people couldn't buy what they wanted in the way of goods and services, they merely postponed or banked their needs and wants and created a pent–up demand that generated pressure throughout the "waiting period" until the war ended and controls were removed.

With the termination of hostilities, the government released production facilities to the private owners. It abolished the War Production Board, which had channeled and scheduled all manufacturing operations, and disbanded the Office of Price Administration, the agency charged with controlling consumer prices and rationing scarce items. At the same time wage controls were withdrawn.

Americans had seethed under the restraints. They had grumbled loudly about their controlled economy, and politicians whose records showed they had never previously given the subject much consideration joined the shout for a return to the private enterprise system.

True, there was a great dammed–up demand for everything ranging from new homes to automobiles to can openers, but the nation's industrial capacity had been nearly doubled by the wartime schedules and there was little doubt that supply could be made to match demand within reasonable time.

That such was the case remains a titanic tribute to the private economy of America. Inflation of prices was held to a minimum of small percentages. Thus the threat of the "classic" inflation was checked.

In Washington, however, and on the campaign soap boxes politicians were wooing the votes of the 12,500,-000 returning American servicemen and their nearly equal number of wives.

"They must return to a better world," was the avowal of the public leaders, and none dared dispute this high aspiration, save the few, immediately branded as ultraconservatives, who suggested that the returning warriors might properly look for individual security and national solvency as the pillars on which to rebuild the stability that was sought by all.

Government services were pyramided throughout the Republic, and as the armed forces were demobilized, the ranks of civil service workers swelled.

In rereading the newspapers of that immediate postwar period, it is now apparent the major theme of government was built around the premise that "the boys won't permit us to have another depression." Implicit in this are two things:

1. The government, itself, is responsible for avoiding depressions, and, ergo, is conversely responsible for causing them, albeit through neglect or omission.

2. Government spending programs are the best defense against depression. This seeming evolvement of the Keynesian pump–priming theory is rooted in the same basic "logic" that was propounded by Lord Keynes.

Thus, instead of decreasing the federal budget at the end of mankind's greatest military conflict, the United States *increased* its budget, its spending, and its indebtedness. Its deficit—the gap between income and outgo —widened with each succeeding year.

It will never be known whether this contributed to fuller employment and greater prosperity than would have been the case under prudent practices and policies, for again, the need for a wartime economy, this time with only partial controls, prevented a showdown with the Keynesian theorists.

The Korean conflict brought about sufficient mobilization of manpower and productive capacity to forestall any accurate measurement of the effects of nonmilitary government programs on the civilian economy.

Again, from Korea to Vietnam was such a short step that any measurement of the benefits or harms of civilian government programs was impractical and inconclusive.

The only real test ever given the pump–priming theory, therefore, was from 1933 to 1940, and then, by impartial judgment, it was a failure, if its purpose was to create jobs and stimulate prosperity. There were as many unemployed at the time war broke out as when the pump priming started, and the nation was no more prosperous than it had been in 1933.

The sole effects that were measurable to any degree were in the pocketbooks of the citizens. The cost of living increased sharply, and the purchasing power of the dollar declined significantly. From 1933 through 1942 the cost of living increased by about 50 per cent on the old charts with the dollars of 1911-1913 representing 100. This meant that the purchasing power of the dollar dropped correspondingly.

Put in proper perspective this meant that $100 in your savings account was worth $50 in what it would buy.

It meant, conversely, that your weekly food bill of $50.00 became $75.00.

The price of a $1,000 automobile increased to at least $1,500, had one been available.

Many economic experts with impressive academic credits told us, to the confusion of some of us, that all of this was good for the economy, that it was progressive, and that it helped a great many Americans who needed the help.

Thus, thirty–five years after it was introduced to the American economy, the pump–priming theory remains unchallenged, a deep–rooted part of American economic philosophy and unalterable dogma to the public officials who are constrained to woo and romance the voters. It is by all odds the best voter–persuading device ever conceived.

Since the mid–1930s there have been some who have cautioned against excessive spending and others who have pointed out that this is a politician–perpetuating gimmick because no one wants to vote against Santa Claus, but they have been shouted down as cynics or nonintellectuals or selfishly motivated conservatives in the employ of the greedy big corporations.

Now, in the 1970s, the academic world and the so–called intellectuals, both the duly delegated and the self–anointed, have activated a project that has been a long–favorite idea of the world's self–styled "progressives."

It is the guaranteed annual wage.

It is simple. It has compelling appeal. And it is being proposed at a time when taxpayers are getting fed up with excessive welfare payments and abuses in the welfare system.

The latest proposal, a guaranteed annual *income*, as opposed to a guaranteed annual *wage*, is a blend of the guaranteed wage sought by the New Left during the Kennedy administration and the negative income tax proposed by Dr. Milton Friedman, economic adviser to Senator Barry Goldwater when he was the unsuccessful presidential candidate in 1964.

According to its supporters, the guaranteed annual income has the endorsement both of a majority of the academic economists and of a great number of business leaders, the corporate custodians whose companies will be required to provide the largest proportion of the tax revenues to pay for the program. These business men, it is said, are convinced that only a guaranteed annual income will ease the nation's tensions over poverty, especially in minority groups, and particularly among Negroes and Puerto Ricans.

In interviews with the author, business leaders gave a variety of reasons for their support of the guaranteed income, but the three most commonly cited—probably in their order of importance—were:

1. A guaranteed annual income will bring an end to the mishmash of localized welfare benefits, many of them conflicting, and none of which seems to solve the problem.

2. It will provide subsistence automatically for a small but significant number among male Negroes who are untrainable and unemployable, and who otherwise would remain on the national conscience.

3. It will end the migration of the impoverished from states and cities with minimum welfare benefits to those with maximum welfare benefits (that is, $10 to $14 per week per *family* in some Southern cities, compared with as much as $3,200 per year for each illegitimate child, under certain conditions, in New York City).

A hope, expressed by several, was that a guaranteed income would be less expensive, in total, than the conglomerate welfare programs. There are no figures to substantiate this, of course, though several claim to be convinced that such would be the case.

There can be no doubt, however, that the guaranteed annual income is being advanced as the ultimate program for stamping out poverty and that many important Americans believe it will do all that its supporters claim for it.

Under the plan, as urged by 1,000 college and university economists, any American who earns less than a predetermined minimum–existence income will receive supplemental money from the government to bring his income up to the fixed level.

At the outset, of course, the minimum–existence income would vary from city to city, depending on how much it costs to live. As of late 1969, the cost of living in Orlando, Florida, was lower than in any other city in the nation. Even though the living–cost factors shift from time to time, it is assumed that if the guaranteed annual income program were in effect at present, those eligible in Orlando would receive less that those in, say, San Francisco or New York, or even Bangor, Maine, where winter fuel and the transportation costs for processed and prepared foods must be taken into consideration.

No specific plan has been advanced—except that the income in each case is to be based on need, in relation to family size. Although a great many of the supporters of the guaranteed income envision it as a replacement for the myriad welfare schemes in existence that are maintained with funds from various levels of government, town, city, county, state and federal, some of the earlier advocates, such as Michael Harrington, articulate essayist for the New Left, as well as members of the Ad Hoc Committee of the Triple Revolution thought of it as being separate and apart from the welfare programs—something that would be superimposed atop welfare and would not disturb the "qualifications" of those now receiving aid or other benefits.

In fact, Mike Harrington envisions the guaranteed annual income as more of a division of the national wealth than as something to end poverty, per se, and believes the time will come when, with the evolution of cybernetics—the science of creating machines to operate the machines that produce—such a distribution of the national wealth will be the only practical means of feeding back into the economy that which is taken from it and produced for it.

When man is no longer required to work because of machines doing most jobs for him, society may regard it as unfair to base a man's wealth on the amount of work he performs, since work will not be of great value.

Farfetched as this dream may seem at the present, it is high on the agenda of the planning that is being done by the intellectuals of the New Left.

It is difficult to sell such an idea in a society that is built on private enterprise and that has a work–oriented culture grounded in the philosophy that work has a special virtue. Most people believe that America's great wealth, and the wealth of other nations, results from hard work that is done because of the desire to be rid of poverty and hunger.

This is true, of course, for it is the end result of the socio–religious doctrines that for centuries have emphasized the exercise of free will and the fact that a man is responsible for his own welfare and that those who work hardest will receive the greatest rewards, as summed up, perhaps too grandly, in "Invictus": "I am the Captain of my Fate; I am the Master of my Soul."

The flaw is that rewarding work is not always available to those who wish to work, and a major fault is that sometimes the easiest work yields the highest rewards, and frequently the hardest work produces the slimmest recompense.

With all of its numerous recognized faults, the existing system may yet be the best, for a cybernated world, where machines run machines that produce wealth, seems just a little too good to be true. Even in Heaven, folks expect to prune their own rose bushes.

Cynics may wonder who will bother to learn how to repair and rebuild the machines once the original builders have died, if there are no greater rewards for working than there are for not working. And who will invent the newer machines of the future, if the rewards are minimized or neutralized? Incentive to earn greater rewards is, and will remain, foremost in prodding mankind to ever greater achievements. Even in the academic world, where the profit motive is so frequently scorned if not spurned, achievement has special rewards of recognition and privilege that substitute for monetary profit, and also quite often accompany it. Ayn Rand's great symbolic novel, *Atlas Shrugged*, obviously made no impression on the intellectuals of Mike Harrington's segment of the New Left.

Nevertheless, as a substitute for the welfare programs, the idea of the guaranteed annual income is gaining support and strength.

The Federal Department of Health, Education and Welfare (HEW) says that the United States has 30 million "poor" people who live substandard existences. Of these, says HEW, about 10 million live in families that have one full-time breadwinner whose income is insufficient to support the family.

The federal government now provides about $8 billion annually in welfare expenditures. At least an equal amount—probably more—is spent by cities, counties and states to supplement the federal appropriation.

In New York City alone, one out of every seven residents receives welfare benefits of some kind—about 1,300,000 people.

No one really knows how much the guaranteed annual income will cost the federal government. Varying estimates have been made, ranging from a low of $11 billion to a high of $26 billion annually. If the $26 billion is a genuine "high" figure and not, indeed, a "low," as is so frequently the case with federal programs, it may be proved in time that this sum is actually less than the total spent by all levels of government on welfare under existing systems. If this turns out to be true, it may not be very difficult to legislate the guaranteed annual income into being.

The nation has been spending $20 billion annually in

waging the Vietnam war. In addition, government economists like to point out that tax revenues increase at a rate of about $10 billion annually—forgetting, of course, that a great portion of the increase accrues from higher prices, or in other words, from inflation. The point is, a great many people, voters and legislators alike, may be led to believe that the federal budget can "afford" the guaranteed annual income, and it may not be as remote as it seems.

It may provide the next major inflationary force.

It may wipe out poverty.

In so doing it may likely wipe out the savings of the vast majority of middle–income Americans.

In time its benefits will be neutralized and recipients with $4,000 or $5,000 or $6,000 a year guaranteed annual income will be no better off than they are now.

And then jobholders in those brackets will join the ranks of the unemployed.

It has been noted by welfare officials that it requires anywhere from $4,500 to $4,700 annually for a family of four to eke out a "bare subsistence" in New York City. If a few years lapse before a guaranteed annual income can become law, then it's rather safe to assume that the rock–bottom minimum in New York City might be $5,-000 for a couple with two children.

This raises a few questions:

Since a breadwinner will have to save $100,000 in order to get a $5,000 income in interest or dividends from a savings account paying 5 per cent annually, why should he work hard to accumulate such a substantial nest egg when he can get precisely the same annual income simply by being willing to be poor? (Oh, can't you hear the hotheads screaming: "Nobody *wants* to be poor!")

Or what about the chap in Kew Gardens who works like a beaver selling men's shoes in Detwiler's store for

$7,500 a year? Won't he feel that he is really working for $2,500 annually, since he can get $5,000 by not working?

What will happen to the not–too–smart, not–too–ambitious fellow who gets $85 a week by spending three hours a night, five nights a week, sweeping the floor of Spiffy Fashions, Inc. on Seventh Avenue? He'll be bright enough, won't he, to figure that by working he's collecting only $4,420 per year, and that by not working he can get $5,000 from the government? Then what machine is there that will do the sweeping in Spiffy Fashions, Inc.? The only "machine" left will be the boss himself, the employer of 3,500 people. Will he do his own sweeping, or will he say, "T'hell with it," and move to Miami Beach to live off his savings, knowing that even if he uses them all up, the government will provide for him?

And what happens to the kid who wants to get ahead and is willing to take a job at Spiffy Fashions, Inc. as floor sweeper at $4,420 a year in order to be in a cutting room where he can learn the business?

In reality, however, the boss will probably figure he can raise his prices somewhat and increase his profits a bit, and pay a higher salary to his sweeper from Kew Gardens.

A raise of $15 a week will bring him to $5,200, and the sweeper, with a wife and two children, will tell the boss that he can't work for a whole year for $200, inasmuch as he can collect $5,000 for not working.

What income will induce the sweeper to sweep? Will $6,000 a year—$1,000 for working five nights a week for fifty weeks a year?

Will $8,000? Or $10,000?

At some point there is a figure over and above the free $5,000 at which the sweeper will be willing to work. At that figure the boss will rehire him.

Let's suppose it's $25 more per week than the fellow

with a wife and two children can get by not working, or $7,500 a year. That's an increase of $3,080 per year for the sweeper, a raise of $65 per week. He produces no more; he contributes no more to the company; thus his raise is totally inflationary.

In Spiffy Fashions, Inc., however, there are 1,000 people whose earnings range from $6,000 per year to $10,-000, based on their acquired skills, their value to the company, their contribution to the total effort and, of course, their length of service, the latter being a factor that may or may not contribute to greater production.

Is a skilled cutter who receives $8,500 a year going to be willing to work for only $1,000 more a year than the unskilled sweeper?

Is the skilled foreman, who is paid $11,000, going to be willing to work for only $3,500 more per year than the unskilled sweeper, and but $6,000 more per year than the unworking welfare recipient, when he stops to think of the years he spent as a student, a scholar, an apprentice, and a learner, finally moving up to journeyman, then assistant foreman, and ultimately to foreman?

Of course not! Anyone who has ever observed the wage patterns in the United States or any country with a free economy knows that a boost in the wages for the lowest paid means a boost in the wages and salaries for all.

Similarly, such wage boosts cause inflation, which quickly wipes out any advantage that the pay raise brought, and soon each worker is buying just exactly as much as he bought before, and no more, even though he is receiving more money for his work.

The general increase benefits only moneylenders. The banks, responding to outworn but unchallenged credit policies, grant larger loans and extend more credit to the employees who have received the pay raises, gambling that the notes will be repaid and satisfied before the backlash of inflation catches up with the dubious "benefits." Bankers know that when most $4,000 employees receive $5,000, no one is any better off. They have a more generous attitude, however, toward the ones who are the first to receive the increases.

The only measurable effect is on the unemployed and the retired, or the previously employed.

When the whole level of national income moves higher, the unemployed must pay more for everything they must buy, including shelter, food and all basic needs. Any predetermined grant from the government will then be rendered worthless in time.

The retired person faces an even more hopeless plight, for usually there is no way he can supplement his income to forestall the erosion of the purchasing power of his fixed number of dollars. He retires on a specific, fixed income that will buy a certain standard of living. When the cost of that standard of living moves higher, it simply leaves him behind. He has to buy a lower standard of living. Then a lower one. And so on, until death. Like Eustace Hathaway.

Facing the future realistically, this is what seems in store for Americans.

There is a bright side, of course. A nation without poverty is a better nation by any measurement.

The trouble is, a guaranteed annual income can only stamp out poverty temporarily. There is a side danger, too, in that the qualities of individual responsibility, free will, and self-determination may be seriously undermined by a life that, temporarily at least, knows no anxiety or fear to hone and develop the sense of responsibility in the individual.

There is really no way to get around the old verity that something you get for nothing is worth . . . nothing.

Yet this, or something like it, is coming. What to do?

How can you prevent your savings from being rendered worthless? How can you insure that the years of hard work you have put in will still reward you fairly? How do you make certain that you will be rewarded for the many times that you worked and were "responsible" while others played, and were indifferent?

The reaction of my friend behind the drugstore counter to the notion of a guaranteed annual income may be noteworthy for those who have not taken into consideration its effect on the full range of human (and institutional) values.

The man who owns the drugstore is a registered pharmacist, but there is simply too much business for one man to handle. He hires my friend and pays him $7,500 a year, with a three–week vacation, Blue Cross and Blue Shield membership, along with other minor benefits including a 10 per cent discount on anything purchased in the store.

"Look," said my friend when we discussed the guaranteed annual income idea, "it would be just right for someone like yourself, a writer. You suffer from fluctuating income and it's almost impossible to plan for book royalties and checks from magazines to arrive on a certain schedule. You have years when you have more money than you really need, and then there are years when you don't have enough.

"But take my case: I have a steady job, a responsible one. I had to go through four years of high school, two years of college and two years at pharmacy school to get my degree and earn my license. I work a forty–eight hour week, at least, and sometimes more, and get, roughly, $150 a week for that skilled work.

"Now if I learn that anyone and everyone can get $4,000 a year for not working and never learning a skill, I'm going to want a great deal more than $7,500."

"How much more?" I asked.

"For me, zero will start at $4,000. I can get $4,000 for not working. Therefore, to pay me relatively the same amount as I'm getting now, I'd need $4,000 more than $7,500—or, $11,500.

"Let me put it another way," he went on. "If my contribution to this society and the economy is worth $7,-500 today, and the reward to those who contribute nothing is zero, the minute you start paying $4,000 a year to those who contribute nothing, my contribution is not any longer worth a mere $3,500 more than that of a noncontributor, it's worth $7,500 more than the noncontributor, or a total of $11,500."

My friend's boss had been leaning on the counter, listening to at least part of our discussion. I turned to him.

"Would you be willing to raise his pay by $4,000 a year?" I asked.

"Well, I wouldn't be *willing*," he said, "but the way I see it, I'd be forced to if I wanted to keep an assistant working here."

There is little doubt that this reaction will be universal.

The outcome, of course, will be rampant, runaway inflation, ruinous to the economy.

If, on the other hand, the politicians should institute a guaranteed annual income and at the same time decree that wages and salaries be frozen during a period of adjustment, forcing my friend to continue to work as a pharmacist for a $7,500 salary worth, in his mind, only $3,500, the condition will be ruinous to individual incentive, that greatest contributing factor to the nation's unprecedented wealth.

Looking at it subjectively, I may consider that as a writer I might fare well in some of my "bad" years. But I am constrained to ask myself the question: How will my country fare?

What may be a wonderful boon to me, may not be best for my countrymen. Surely inflation, which must result from a guaranteed income, is the most harmful and hurtful of all taxes.

Moreover, it is quite likely that as a nation we miss the point entirely in our attempt to solve one of the major problems of poverty.

While there are, indeed, many Americans who are actually hungry and are, in fact, woefully housed, for whom help must be forthcoming without hesitation, the greatest proportion of the so-called impoverished, or those living in substandard conditions, do not need money as much as they need credit.

We confuse the two. Strangely, it seems especially to confuse the "experts."

When we list the "lacks" among the poor people—the things they like and the things they actually need—we speak of better homes, better furnishings, better clothes, a car, a television set, a chance to get higher education. These are no longer luxuries. They are virtually necessities, today. Even a television set is a necessity if it keeps the kids off the streets.

We are not discussing cash items, however. We are discussing things that are bought on credit.

The experts persist in regarding ours as a "consumer society," when in fact it's only partly that. Mostly it's a credit society. The whole economy is functioning on credit, and indebtedness of frightening dimensions exists for the federal government, for every lesser government, and for all American individuals from the richest down to the low level of the middle-income bracket. There it ends. Those who exist beneath that level are poor not because they lack cash, but because they lack credit.

Credit is partly determined by the policies that affect the banking community as set down by the Federal

Reserve Board. After that it is self-managed and amateurishly policed, with the result that this most important single element of economic existence is left in the hands of incompetents ranging, in many cases, from boobs to dolts.

Nevertheless, because of basic policies formulated long ago, when the business world was smaller and keener judgment was used instead of computers, credit is extended not because of the amount of cash an applicant has, or the expected size of his income, but because of his proven or demonstrated responsibility. Responsibility is the key to all credit.

Responsibility cannot be legislated. It cannot be disguised as a check and mailed out from Washington. It cannot be granted to deserving people by well-wishers in city hall. It is as elusive as Maeterlinck's bluebird of happiness, as impossible to pin down as a poltergeist, yet it is as specific and measurable as a gallon of gasoline.

Responsibility can only be self-attained; and then it can only be self-demonstrated.

It is here that the credit system falls down, for it has become so large that it is guided by "averages" and "norms" and is totally computerized. Worse, it is run by clerks who are untrained for little else, who are unknowing about the nuances of credit, who lose all sight of the individual.

Prejudice plays a strong role in the issuance of credit, and it is here that the minorities have their strongest and most justified complaint, if they could only be made to realize it. It is *assumed* that responsibility is less prevalent in the ghettos—which may or may not be true since no one has ever sought or studied that vitally important statistic—hence a man's color and his address play an important part in his application for credit. A colored man in Harlem has to *prove* his responsibility much more thoroughly, and with more explicit documentation, than does the white Anglo–Saxon Protestant of Greenwich, Connecticut, or the well–dressed Jew on Park Avenue.

But the cruelest credit practices are run by independent, unregulated, unsupervised credit agencies and credit-reporting bureaus.

The inhuman abuses perpetrated on their fellowmen by the credit reporters are legion—and totally ignored, for no law controls them, and no regulatory body supervises them. They serve long lists of "clients," usually retailers and professional men such as doctors, dentists, optometrists, who pay the reporters either an annual fee or a "per action" fee, or both, to research and report on the credit "rating" of an individual.

This rating is inspecific, unstandardized, and quite likely to be varied in each agency as one eager beaver or another improvises on some imaginary scale calculated to reveal the credit potential of any one person.

It is all pure hogwash.

The most unforgivable practice among these "professional" credit reporters is their failure to update their research, along with their refusal to throw away old records and periodically clear out their files.

Such practices should be mandatory, of course, but they are not. Lawmakers are only now beginning to realize that this is a credit society, rather than a consumer's society, and they feel that a long progressive stride has been made with passage of the so–called Truth in Lending law. It is truly but a beginning.

Arthur Lothan, a Negro, of St. Albans, Queens, New York, was a hard–working, responsible citizen, married and the father of three children, the eldest nine, the youngest three. He worked for fourteen years as an asphalt mixer and paver, and earned a good, steady income. He was buying a house on credit, a car on credit, numerous appliances on credit, and had been granted a modest personal loan at his bank to take a vacation and take his family to his home town in Texas to see his parents.

One Sunday afternoon, when Arthur was fishing for striped bass off the high rocks near Fort Totten at the western end of Long Island Sound where it meets the East River, he slipped and fell, striking his head on a boulder several feet below. He was discovered by other fishermen who called the police. Later he was transferred to a hospital.

It was nearly six months before Arthur really regained consciousness and during the period, two operations had been performed to remove pressure and bone chips from the brain. It was a year before he could think of returning to work.

During his illness, his home had been foreclosed, his car had been repossessed, his furniture and furnishings had been sold, and, because of failure to repay his personal loan, his bank had brought a legal judgment against him. It was pending and "hot," since there was nothing left on which to place a lien.

His wife and children had moved in with relatives, and Mrs. Lothan worked nights as a waitress to help pay for room and board.

Arthur returned to his job just as quickly as he could. His pay was a little higher than when he had left, for the pay scale had moved up during his absence. The boss appreciated his experience, however, and made no trouble about finding a place for Arthur.

He needed a car to get to work. He tried to buy one, and filled out a credit application form for the salesman, who assured him there would be no trouble at all. Two days later he was informed he couldn't have the car; his credit rating was very bad.

After some months of skimping, Arthur bought a car

for cash, and was, so to speak, "back in business." He and his family were renting a small apartment not far from where he formerly lived.

Two years later he had enough money on hand for a down–payment on a modest house. He found the house he wanted, and applied for a mortgage.

It was denied after a credit search had been made.

Arthur had a bad credit record.

The truth was, however, that Arthur was a most responsible man. He had a *good* credit record. It became bad when he was in the hospital, unemployed. The records were not purged. No one took into account his restoration to his previous good standing. All that seemed to count was that he previously had a bad credit experience. No one took into account, either, the fact that Arthur now had more assets than ever before. He had paid cash for his television set, cash for his furniture, cash for his rugs, cash for his appliances. These were all good, hard assets, and belonged to him exclusively, unconditionally, and unencumbered.

Arthur's co–workers, many of whom make less money, and quite a few of whom are much less responsible about their debts, have no trouble buying the things they need on "time." They can get credit easily.

Arthur still is unable to buy that new home he wants.

Arthur is a bitter man.

The same thing happens at the other end of the scale, too. A friend of mine, second in command of a large advertising agency, lost his job because of a merger. From $100,000 a year, his salary dropped to zero. It stayed there for three years while he pounded the pavements on Madison Avenue, looking for another "top job."

He lost his home in Westchester—and his car, and everything else that wasn't nailed down. Now he's getting $90,000 a year again, and he can't get credit enough to buy a pair of blue jeans in his local cut-rate chain store.

With him it isn't so tough. He has a large roll of cash to buy what he needs. With Arthur Lothan, it's different. He needs his cash, for he *lives* on credit. And he has none.

This is not a digression. It is a condition that is deeply involved in any consideration of the problem of poverty, and the high cost of battling poverty in America is one of the chief contributing factors to the eroding inflation that eats at the nation's vitals.

Clearly, credit reporting must be made more scientific on the one hand, and more humanized on the other. Standards and norms must be set. Old records must be purged and destroyed, and new ones created. Careful control must be exercised over such records, as to who sees them, who has access to them.

For a fee, in some communities, anyone can check on any credit rating, if only out of curiosity, and that, no matter how it's disguised, is an invasion of privacy.

There are some things the computers can never know, and some things the credit raters may be incapable of learning, all of which bear strongly on the situation.

When Arthur O. Deitz was chief executive officer of the giant lending institution now known as Universal C.I.T. Credit Corporation, he never brought legal action to recover money on a defaulted note; yet, he told this writer, in all his years there, defalcations, which many regarded as ultimately collectable, ran to only one–half of one per cent. When A. P. Giannini headed his banking operation in California, he resolved never to bring legal action against a delinquent loan. His Bank of America is now the second largest bank in the nation.

But how to tell that to an IBM machine, or to a programmer who could never have the vision or wisdom of a Deitz or a Giannini?

The one unforgivable crime in America is to be poor. It is permissible to be impoverished and totally under-privileged, for in this condition you can be the recipient of many governmental programs and much charitable do–goodery. The great crime is to be self–sufficient and poor, independent and poor, taxpaying and poor.

If you fall into that category you are an object of society's contempt and the establishment's scorn. Everybody in the corporate world knows that the lower paid in a two-man department merits lesser respect. He also gains the slimmer credit rating.

It is up the scale a little way, however, that credit reporting and credit evaluating can cause the bread-winner enormous problems. As he moves up the pay scale, his living costs increase, frequently on an obliga-tory basis, commensurate with his rising "position" in his company and in his community. He finds it neces-sary to buy higher–priced items carrying big price tags —a better home, a bigger car, better furniture and fur-nishings (for he must entertain), more expensive clothes for himself and his wife, higher club dues, big-ger restaurant and bar tabs.

As he climbs the commercial and social ladder, though his income increases, he leans more and more heavily on his credit.

Part of this is due to inflation, for the "better things of life" keep costing more; part is due to his success and his need to back it up with material evidence, an in-stinctive act of shoring up and bulwarking his progress.

He has ceased to be a consumer—he is a credit con-sumer; without credit he will be no consumer, for his income is fully committed.

Strange as it seems, this man needs protection—legal protection—from the credit evaluators and credit reporters. By a careless but arbitrary statement about his "credit record," some clerk in a credit–reporting bureau or in a finance company can ruin this man's career, shut off his credit, create a needless stampede of bill collectors and cause all manner of hell and harassment.

This happened to a friend of mine. Let's call him Walt.

He worked in the sales department of a prominent electronic engineering technical corporation, one of the corporate conglomerates, in Fairfield County, Connecticut. The firm he had worked for since graduating from college was absorbed by the larger company, and he was transferred to the head office in Connecticut where, in short order, his superiors decided he was just the man they wanted to groom for the top spot in his division.

Accordingly, he was promoted and promoted again, and his salary was sweetened periodically. He was encouraged to move into one of the better and more expensive neighborhoods of Fairfield County, and to take an active part in community life, which, of course, meant joining one of the more costly country clubs. For good measure he acquired a small cabin cruiser so that he might qualify for yacht club membership.

Soon it became no secret that Walt was also being groomed for a vice presidency and the top sales job in the whole corporation.

Walt is not a show–off. He is basically a quiet man, but he has all the qualities of a crack salesman. He's also top–notch at planning campaigns and administering them.

The move to richer quarters and the membership in the clubs and acquisition of possessions were all, to him, just part of the job, essential to his career.

Credit, to him, was just as necessary as it is to General Motors. Without it he couldn't "expand" to meet his growing "market." The bigger, better life, to Walt, was merely the means to a bigger, better income—precisely as a bigger investment to General Motors is the means to bigger profits.

Instead of dealing with professional credit people in the highest banking levels, as do the officials of General Motors, Walt merely went ahead and took advantage of numerous charge accounts, budget plans, and small installment loans that were made available as he needed them.

Then a series of events happened that shattered the entire career of this promising young executive.

First was the matter of his son's car. In Connecticut a youth can drive at sixteen years of age, and in Walt's neighborhood, few boys of that age were without "wheels."

When Walt's boy Joel first began asking for a car of his own, Walt pleaded poverty—he just couldn't afford one then, he said, particularly when he considered the extra amount of insurance needed for an underage driver.

The apple doesn't fall far from the tree, and young Joel has a great many of his old man's qualities. Like his father, he considered a "no" as the first part of a sale. He changed his tactics.

First he attended a Driver Education course in his school, which, upon completion, gave him a special rate with the insurance companies, thus lowering the premium. Then he went out and got a real job in a supermarket, working after school and early evenings Monday through Friday, and all day Saturday until 9:00 P.M. He was making enough money to buy his own car —and of course there was one all picked out in a used-car lot.

Joel sought an audience with his dad and presented

his case. He even had a letter from his boss in the super-market stating that Joel was a good worker and his services would be in continued demand there on the basis of Joel's past and present performance of his duties. He exhibited a savings bank passbook with a balance that was more than sufficient to make a down–payment on the car of his dreams.

Joel wanted to buy and pay for his own car. He wanted to pay for his own insurance. He had a job that would permit him to do so.

Walt really had no choice but to praise his son for his industriousness, and to tell him he could get the car. He was proud of his boy and permitted himself to reflect that he was a lot like the old man and would be a howling success one day, too. Joel didn't ask for favors; he was willing to pay his own way.

Accordingly, Joel rushed off to buy his car. He returned with some papers for Walt to fill out and sign. It was a strange credit application form, handled through one of those finance companies that specialize in automobile loans. Since Joel was under legal age, Walt had to take the loan in his own name. Legally the car would belong to him, and he, Walt, would be responsible for its loan payments. Technically, the car would belong to Joel and he would provide the money for payments. It was the same with the insurance. Walt had to insure the car, and it was listed as "Vehicle Number 3" in his policy (Walt's wife had car number 2) but Joel paid the premium directly to his father.

Joel got his car with no difficulty. When the payment "book" arrived from the finance company, Walt proudly turned it over to his enterprising son, with instructions to make monthly payments to Walt's wife, who handled the household bills. She would write a check each month for the finance company.

When the matter was settled, Walt dismissed it from

his mind. He was a busy man with many more pressing matters to consider. He knew there was no reason to worry about Joel and his car payments.

About six months later, at the height of the winter social season, the chairman of the board of Walt's company invited Walt and his wife to visit for ten days at his mansion in one of Florida's most exclusive and expensive resorts. Needless to say, Walt and his wife accepted with great pleasure and anticipation. It was obvious that this portended great things for Walt's future. The board chairman was not given to uncommon affability, even with the highest–ranking officials of the company.

For two weeks prior to their departure, Walt and Evelyn engaged in a protracted spending spree, completely outfitting themselves in resort clothes, sports clothes, evening wear, beach wear and—since they knew a boat trip was in the offing—cruise wear.

Before they left they had to arrange with their two–day–a–week cleaning woman to become a full–time housekeeper, so she could take care of the place during their absence. In addition, they had to buy a round–trip plane fare from Los Angeles so that Evelyn's mother could be flown to Connecticut to stay with the kids. Evelyn also made two trips to Joel's supermarket to load the refrigerator, pantry and freezer, so there would be no crises over food or groceries while she was away.

Their visit was scheduled for the middle of February. Knowing they'd need plenty of cash on their vacation, Walt and Evelyn had decided not to pay any of their January bills and to deposit only a small portion of Walt's salary check. Also, they had decided they'd utilize their Diners' Club, American Express and Carte Blanche credit cards as fully as possible.

They decided to drive to Florida, figuring that their

car might be needed there, thus extending their vacation by six days—three days down, three back.

"Besides," Evelyn explained to her mother, "if you go by plane you never know whether you'll be hijacked to Cuba, and if you go by rail you're made to feel most unwanted."

Never will Walt and Evelyn forget their Florida visit. The board chairman greeted them by explaining that when he worked, he was all business, but when he relaxed, he made a business out of relaxing. He presented the couple to his wife who proved to be charming, witty, attractive, and a most considerate and thoughtful hostess.

Each day was packed with pleasure and enjoyment. About every other night at a formal dinner, either in their host's home or at a posh club or restaurant, the chairman would introduce Walt to some impressively important people whose names Walt instantly recognized from the business and financial pages of the *New York Times* and *Wall Street Journal.*

When it came time to leave, the host and hostess urged Walt and Evelyn to stretch it out for another week, but Walt, instinctively aware of the nuances of super salesmanship, knew when to back off and leave the customer asking for more. He pleaded pressure of work back at the office.

Standing under the portico, just before they drove off, the chairman wrung Walt's hand and clapped him on the shoulder, saying, "I'm sure glad you're crewing on our team, Walt. I think you have a great future with our outfit."

"Thank you, sir. I'll do my best."

"That's good enough for me."

Walt wore a grin all the way home.

"Evelyn," he kept saying, "we've got it made."

In North Carolina the car broke down. Crankshaft,

pinion, and other things, the mechanic said. It could be repaired to serve for a while, but Walt would be wise to trade it in, was the advice.

As they resumed their northward trip after a two–day delay, Walt's high spirits returned. "Who cares about a car?" he asked. "We'll buy a half–dozen."

Nothing specific was said, but Walt had his eye on the presidency of the company. The chairman had alluded repeatedly to the fact that the company had "passed through" its technical research and development period, and its legal–tax–merger phase, and now the day was at hand to concentrate heavily on sales. Walt knew also that the incumbent president, a former tax lawyer, was as rich as the board chairman, had passed his sixtieth birthday, and might possibly be looking toward retirement or semiretirement.

Two days after his return he drove his ailing car to the agency where he had bought it two years before. He looked over the floor models and consulted the brochures. He settled at last on a heavy, powerful model, fully equipped with all the latest devices and gadgets. He made out the order under the tutelage of an obsequious salesman, and filled out the credit application form, which was directed to one of the local banks.

Walt went whistling off to his job.

Two days later he received a call at his office from the car salesman. He was no longer obsequious. He was blunt, to the point.

"Your application for credit has been turned down," he said.

"Wh–what? How in hell can that be?"

"I don't know, sir. All I know is that the bank says no."

"Why, that's impossible. I'll find out about this. I'll get back to you."

"Very good, sir. We'll just hold up this order until we hear from you."

He had barely hung up when his secretary entered his office.

"There's a man here to see you."

"Who is he?"

His secretary looked a bit smug. "He's a deputy sheriff."

"Okay. Send him in."

"I'm sorry to do this, sir," said the law's minion, who was really anything but sorry, since he was paid a fee for serving such papers, "but I must present you with this writ of attachment."

"Just what the hell IS this," demanded Walt, getting angry.

"It is an attachment on your checking account, sir. The finance company . . . the used car you bought seven months ago . . ."

Walt called his bank and spoke to the manager.

"Yes," said the manager, "your account is attached. We can't pay any checks. Until this is removed, any checks that you write will be returned with the notation that the account has been attached."

"But I wrote a check to a garage in North Carolina, and to a motel in Georgia, and there were a couple of checks we wrote yesterday," Walt protested.

"I'm sorry. They'll be returned." The manager was crisp, formal, anything but the affable friendly fellow who had welcomed Walt as a customer when he first moved to the town.

"There *has* to be some mixup. I'll straighten it out."

"Yes." The banker sounded disbelieving.

Walt called the finance company and asked to speak to the manager. He was a local man, head of the local office, one of more than a thousand branch offices around the country. Walt identified himself, then demanded to know what on earth was going on.

"You're two months behind in your payments on the car," the manager told him.

"For this you'd attach my checking account? How much is involved?"

"Two payments at $34.82 apiece, plus late charges of $1.74 on each payment, let's see, that comes to $73.12."

It was at this point that an exasperated and frustrated Walt made his big mistake. He lost his temper.

"Why you little two–bit bastard," roared Walt, "d'you mean to tell me you'd attach my account for a lousy seventy–three dollars?"

"Seventy–three dollars AND twelve cents—yes, sir, we would, under the circumstances."

"What do you mean, 'under the circumstances'?"

"You don't have a very good credit rating, sir. We don't consider you a very good risk." It was obvious that the manager was enjoying himself. He relished his role of making the mighty squirm.

"By god," Walt stormed, "that's the best one yet! I'll bet I make five times the income you do!"

"Perhaps that's so, sir, but I pay my bills."

"Well, so do I."

"We have not found that to be the case."

"You'll be paid. You'll be paid today," Walt shouted, and slammed down the phone.

He was about to pick up the phone and call Evelyn and tell her to write a check immediately and send it to the finance company, when the realization struck him that he couldn't write a check. How on earth *could* he make his payments?

He called the finance company again.

"Say," he told the manager, "I want to send you a check for $73.12, but you'll have to tell me how I go about it. You've got my account attached."

"I would suggest that you have your lawyer handle

it," the manager said. "Have him authorize the bank to pay us from your attached account. He has the proper legal papers. Incidentally, it is for the full amount of the loan."

"Wh–what! You said $73.12."

"Yes, but if you'll read your contract, we may demand the full amount of the loan if you fail to keep up the payments."

That was that.

Walt called his lawyer and made arrangements to free his checking account. The lawyer had to lend Walt some cash so he could buy groceries over the weekend. The final settlement cleaned out his account.

There was still the matter of the new car. Walt explained the situation to his lawyer, relating that his credit had been denied.

"That's the finance company," the lawyer said. "They must have given you a bad report. Did you list the finance company among your creditors when you filled out the credit application?"

"Of course. It says you have to list all creditors."

"Yes—well, obviously that same manager told the bank you were a bad risk."

"But I'm NOT a bad risk," Walt exclaimed. "What can we do?"

"Well, you can apply at a different bank, now, and you won't have to list the finance company as a creditor— you've paid 'em off."

"But the credit application specifically asks if you have had any credit applications denied in the last year. I'll have to say that I did. Why don't we try to explain the situation to the bank where this auto dealer does business, where my application was denied?"

So the lawyer called the loan officer.

"We just couldn't grant him credit for that much," said the official. "We have his record here—he's two months behind in his mortgage payments; he hasn't paid any of his utility bills in two months; he is two months behind at two department stores; his checking account was recently attached, and we have a record from a finance company that shows that in seven months he made only one payment on time and is now two months delinquent. He has a very bad rating."

The lawyer relayed this information to Walt.

"Well, of course," Walt explained. "We did that deliberately, so I could get a promotion and make a hell of a lot more money. My goodness, isn't my credit good for even two months?"

"Apparently it would have been if it hadn't been for the bad record at the finance company. That tipped over the applecart."

"But it's a *good* record, all but the last two months."

"No, it isn't. You were delinquent on all but one of the payments."

It was then that Walt learned what had happened. The loan for Joel's car had been executed on the fifth of the month, therefore all subsequent payments were due on the fifth of the month. Under the contract he was allowed ten days of grace, but if the monthly installment was unpaid by the fifteenth, he would be declared delinquent.

As a high–ranking officer of his company, Walt was not on the employees' payroll, but rather on an executive payroll. He was given his salary check for the month on the first Wednesday following the fifteenth of the month. After deposits were made, Evelyn set aside a day, anytime within the following week, to sit down and write the checks to pay the bills.

Even though payment had been made every month, the finance company regarded Walt as a delinquent. Accustomed to doing business with wage earners with much lower income than Walt's, the employees at the finance company chalked Walt up as a deadbeat and gave his account a very black mark. The one payment that had been made on schedule was a sheer accident.

Walt then went to his own bank to try to borrow the money to get his new car.

He was turned down flat. Angered because of the injustice of the situation, he had sharp words for the manager.

When he went back to the bank to make his mortgage payments, he was informed that a lien had been placed against the title to his home.

He called his lawyer again, who went to city hall and checked the records. The lien had been placed by the builder who had constructed Walt's new home and who held a second mortgage for a few thousand dollars at a high rate of interest. Walt didn't have to pay off the principal until two more years, but he was supposed to pay the interest monthly. It, too, was two months behind schedule because of his Florida trip.

When the fact of the lien was published in the local newspaper, the department store where Walt and Evelyn did the bulk of their shopping placed another attachment on his checking account.

His superiors at work had spotted the item in the paper, too. Walt was called on the carpet by none less than the board chairman.

Falteringly he explained what had happened, and as he unfolded the story for his boss, he grew angrier and angrier to think he had been ensnared in such an invisible web, and was boxed in by shadows he couldn't fight.

"The trouble is," he concluded, "I have a good job; I earn enough money to pay all of my bills. They just want them paid all at once. Everybody decided to demand payment at the same time—all because of that little worm at the finance company that gave us the loan for Joel's car."

The chairman smiled.

"Relax, Walt," he said, "we can work out an arrangement where you can get an advance on your salary for three months, and pay them all off."

"Gee, that's just wonderful of you."

"Yes, but Walt—we don't like our executives getting into this kind of a mess. You're a friend, so I'll give you a tip. Why don't you start looking around for another job. You're a good man with a lot of promise. Why don't you try to get another start somewhere else." The chairman wasn't asking a question. He was making a statement. He sighed. He was disappointed.

A few days later Walt called the manager of the finance company. He told him what had happened.

"I just had to let you know what you did, my friend," Walt said.

"We didn't have a choice," the manager explained. "We figured that if we gave you a clean bill, you'd have bought a big new car costing a lot of money, and we might never have got the money you owed us."

"But dammit, man, I've never defaulted on payment of a bill in my whole life—that's what I've been trying to tell you right along."

"We don't know about that, sir. All we have to go on is the record. Your record here was a poor one.

"You know, sir," continued the manager, falling back on the incredibly false cliché of all credit raters, "we don't make your credit rating—you do."

Walt sat by the phone and cried.

Walt was a victim of inflation and the mismanaged credit economy that it has spawned.

He's working now for a small firm in the Middle South. He has never climbed all the way out of the hole into which he was tossed by the clerk–manager–credit evaluator in a small–town branch office of a chain finance company, who demanded payment in full of a bill totaling $714.88 that couldn't be paid immediately by a man who was earning nearly $50,000 a year.

There is a lesson here for the politicians looking for new legislation to write. I don't know where a legislator can find a subject needing more thorough study, unless it's a study of the subject of inflation itself.

5. *The Promise*

vs. *the Dream*

Every American political candidate since George Washington, who felt no constraint to burden his administration with commitments, has promised the American voters an elusive and indefinable condition called "economic progress."

Presumably each has meant that there will be growth of the economy, along with general prosperity, but without inflation. None, so far as historical and newspaper accounts show, has ever pledged to cheapen the value of money or to boost prices. Since the administration of William Howard Taft, however, only two Presidents, the recalcitrant Calvin Coolidge and the conservative and stable Herbert Hoover, have been able to maintain steady price levels and a consistent purchasing power in the dollar.

Economic progress, however, is the basic commitment that every politician in every country must make to the voters, though obviously some politicians take the pledge more seriously than do others.

It is important to every single resident of a country, be he voter, taxpayer or mere transient; to every job-holder, for it provides more and better job opportunities; to every breadwinner, for it increases the well-being of all families and protects the value of family savings acquired by thrift, labor or acumen; to every consumer, for true economic progress raises the *real* income, the basic purchasing power; to every investor, for it provides more and better investments while strengthening their safety and enhancing their yield.

In a world scarred by wars and troubled by weak or fluctuating monetary and economic systems, it is more important than ever to American citizens that we maintain what the politicians generalize as economic progress.

The trouble is, we haven't done so with any consistency since 1932.

Ideologically speaking, from the farthest Left to the farthest Right there is not much difference in the broad goals sought under this general term of "economic progress."

With minor differences, they fall into four categories:

1. Economic growth.

2. Minimum unemployment; maximum or "full" employment.

3. A high level of "prosperity"—money in every pocket, so to speak.

4. Stable prices—or *no* inflation.

It is item number four that causes the greatest problem, when the other three goals have been achieved or are in the process of being achieved.

As we near the twenty-first century of the Christian

era and after something like ten thousand years of social experience, the question remains: can we have
these first three desirable objectives without giving up
the fourth?

This is the point, basically, at which the economists
divide their camps and embark on divergent philoso-
phies.

There is really little difference of opinion on the first
three objectives, no matter on what ideological side of
the fence an economist or politician or labor leader or
business man may be found.

Some say we cannot have the first three goals without a little bit of inflation.

Some say that inflation, of any degree, negates—nul-
lifies—attainment to the first three goals.

Some say inflation cannot be avoided if we are to seek
the first three goals.

Some say there is no need for any inflation in our
economy.

We, the ordinary folks, the so–called little people to
whom the politicians make their promises and in
whose behalf the economists of the Right, Left and
Center engage in their academic debates, have three
obligations to ourselves:

1. To recognize the exact extent of the disastrous
effect of inflation on our lives and livelihoods.

2. To realize that inflation has been mounting all
during this century, with the exception of the depression years, and has been deliberately accelerated during the last two decades.

3. To decide what we are going to do about it, first as
concerned citizens, and then as independent individuals who wish to be responsible for our own security and
that of our families.

We must learn to recognize the forces that cause inflation and to anticipate them.

Having done so, we must learn how to avoid being hurt by inflation.

Briefly, let's analyze those three desired goals.

Economic Growth

Population increase. This is one meaning of growth. It is a growth factor that the United States has in abundance. But does it produce a stronger, healthier economy? In a consumer's economy, an enlarging population is helpful, for it creates more consumers. We do not know, yet, whether the same holds true in the credit economy that distinguishes the American system from all others. Indications are that it is not wholly beneficial.

A large population is desirable from a military standpoint in a troubled world, but without economic strength and support it is of dubious value.

A population mass, in itself, may be more harmful to a nation's economy than otherwise. Until China imposed harsh Communistic controls over all its people, and set absolute production schedules and output goals, that most populous nation on earth was the poorest. India, second most populous, has been nearly as poor.

Living standards. These are a more accurate measurement of growth. They are determined by an increase in the rising level of *real* per capita incomes. Living standards are erroneously measured many times by a rise in *gross* per capita incomes—which may mean nothing if prices also rise—or by an increase in the purchasing power of per capita incomes, which inaccurately reflects the economy's health. Such incomes might increase greatly, but actually purchase only slightly more because of attendant price increases, or they might remain static and yet purchase

more because of a drop in prices caused either by
depression or deflation or both.

Output. It is seen, then, that living standards increase as the result of growth in per capita output and
national output.

*In every sense, higher per capita and national out-
put brings higher per capita and national incomes.*

*In every sense, higher per capita income brings a
higher standard of living for the masses of people,* provided it's *real* income and not *inflated* income.

Employment

Full or nearly full employment (jobs for most em-
ployables who want to work) is another definition of
prosperity. When there is full employment, steady employment, and high personal earnings, we are prosperous as individuals and as a nation.

This high level of employment must be accompanied
by a low level of involuntary unemployment, with
minimum and only infrequent periods of unemployment due to layoffs. The low end of the business cycle
in each instance will be brief, so that depressions or
recessions will not have a chance to form and menace
the living standard.

Prosperity

The real meaning of prosperity in the modern American sense is not merely money in almost every pocket
—it is *more* money in almost every pocket.

If, in fact, it could be guaranteed that involuntary
unemployment could be wiped out in its entirety by
rolling back all individual personal incomes to their

1950 level, and by reducing prices by the same ratio, Americans would refuse to do it. Full, maximum employment no longer means prosperity. Prosperity has come to mean the fullest possible employment *plus* an increase in personal incomes.

A clue to what has happened to our "consumer's economy" lies in one of the reasons why Americans would not be willing to give up their 1970–1971 incomes for the same income earned in 1950, even if assured that by doing so they would totally eliminate involuntary unemployment. *They could not do so because of their debt structure.*

Quite simply, they owe too much money; they couldn't live with substantial pay cuts.

As incomes have increased, so has individual indebtedness. So has the availability of credit, including the long–term variety.

It's all part of what we now call prosperity, but it is part and parcel of the uncontrollable inflation that ravages alike the income, the savings and the investments of modern Americans.

By the end of July 1968, installment debt in the United States stood at an all-time high.

The changed American attitude might be better appreciated by recalling the way John D. Rockefeller, Sr. felt about such things. When someone chided him, such a very rich man, for giving a dime tip, he stopped, mildly appraised his audacious critic, and said, "Young man, that dime represents the interest for two entire years on a dollar invested at 5 per cent."

A 5 per cent return on investments in those days was uncommonly high. More likely it represented the dividends or interest of a dollar invested from three and one-half to four years. Of course, "Them as has, gits," and Mr. Rockefeller no doubt had access to better investments than did most people.

There is general agreement that inflation is bad. The disagreement comes over just how bad it is. If anyone had asked Eustace Hathaway, he would have said it ranks with cancer or the plague in its badness. Among the more modern economists, particularly those who manage to influence politicians, a significant number of editors, and the liberal–anointed literati, there are many who say that while inflation is bad, it really isn't disastrously bad. It must be remembered that most of them lead rather sheltered lives in the groves of academe and face the prospect of pensions that will be adjusted to inflation's effects by the decision of other academicians who toil in the same peaceful and bland vineyard and who will receive the same pensions, more or less, depending on their academic achievements.

Inflation is measured usually by a rise in the general level of commodity prices when it is accompanied by a reciprocal decline in the purchasing power of the dollar. In brief, it takes more dollars to buy fewer necessities.

At least four times in American history there has been inflation caused by scarcity—during and after the Civil War, during and after the Spanish–American War, during World War I and during World War II.

Inflation that is induced by scarcities, while dangerous and hurtful, has a predictable terminal point. You know that when the war is ended and the industrial and agricultural capacity is not being drained by military priorities and there are free imports and exports, there will be an end to the condition called inflation where there are too many dollars seeking to purchase an insufficient supply of goods.

Inflation that is caused by imprudent monetary practices and improvident spending habits is quite different, however. It is not—repeat, is *not*—cured by having the government provide a greater number of dollars, or by increasing the supply of purchasable items. That merely compounds the condition, causing deeper inflationary aggravations, and greater declines in the dollar's purchasing power. Improvidence is not corrected by accelerated improvidence. An individual with impractical spending habits who finds himself overwhelmingly in debt does not remedy his problem by going deeper into debt.

These homely and simple verities, accepted as basic by every breadwinner and homemaker, are hotly contended, disputed, debated, at the government level by both politicians and respected economists.

While the debates progress, the Eustace Hathaways of the nation helplessly watch their accumulated savings, their sole hold on liberty and independence, drained away by higher prices and rising taxes and a declining value of the dollars they have invested or saved.

They ask a simple question: Is this economic progress?

The one thing with which all economists agree is that an increase in productivity increases *real* income and advances the standard of living.

It would seem a simple matter, then, if we want a higher rate of prosperity, merely to push for higher per capita productivity—urge every worker to yield just a little more, in product or service, each day. One would expect that citizens and statesmen alike would be waging continuous campaigns to achieve greater output. One might expect that civic organizations, trade associations, unions, the National Association of Manufacturers, and even the schools would be hard at work on plans to boost productivity.

It just doesn't work that way, however.

Many individuals do strive to bolster their output. The self-employed do, if they want more income. Those in the corporate world who seek recognition from superiors so they might be awarded higher salaries, do. Farmers do. Professional men do.

There are vast numbers, though, who are apathetic, indifferent, ignorant, restricted by work rules, or lacking in comprehension of the economic facts of life.

In addition, there are many factors that limit productivity. A truck driver may drive only so far and only so fast without endangering lives. His equipment may carry only so much weight. He cannot increase productivity, if he is working at the maximum. The same holds true of an airline pilot. He is allowed to fly only a certain number of hours each month; after that his safety factor diminishes. His equipment also has fixed capacities. Any number of similar cases can be cited.

There are five other factors that weigh heavily on the output or productivity of a nation, not all subject to an individual's control.

Most important among these is the state of technology—its degree of sophistication. This influences everything else. It, more than anything else, has provided the United States with its economic leadership over the rest of the world.

Technological sophistication is not new to America, nor to Canada. The New World began to surpass the Old World technologically soon after it was settled. The residents of the North American continent began by developing superior, easier-to-use hand tools for the farm, and commenced almost immediately to advance the techniques of organic farming (learned in its crudest form from the supposedly ignorant Indians), which resulted in more abundant crops—greater productivity on a per capita basis.

The North Americans conquered as much of the open seas as they wanted by building technically superior ships and training technically superior officers and crews. As soon as sluiceways and dams harnessed the waterpower and waterwheels were installed, North Americans embarked on programs of rapid industrial technological advancement that rounded out the basic economic strength and gave rise to the capital markets that have, in turn, successively financed the great technological advancements of modern times.

Involved in this was the second factor—natural resources. This includes land, seas, minerals, climate, water, timber, and their accessibility. Without the water, the timber, the rich land, the metals and an invigorating climate, North Americans might not have been off and running with so much economic vigor so early in their history.

However, the factor of natural resources is frequently exaggerated. Two very poor nations with vast natural resources are China and Brazil. Two very well–to–do nations with skimpy natural resources are Switzerland and Norway.

The difference lies in the quality of the human factor. Human resources are much more important than natural resources. This is well to remember, for it means that output and productivity *can* be determined by human effort. This doesn't necessarily mean individual effort.

The other factors controlling productivity include: the quantity and type of capital goods (one tractor can plow a longer furrow than two dozen strong men with spading forks); the quality of workers, their skill, training, dependability, attitude and health; and the number of competent and skilled business managers. (The most skilled workers in the world will dissipate their production unless it is properly scheduled, channeled, computed, packaged, distributed, accounted, and sold.)

Human resources, it can be seen, are of even greater importance than natural resources.

What has really bothered the nation's leaders and its more thoughtful citizens in the last half of the decade of the sixties has been the fear that the nation is depleting its human resources, just as it is depleting some natural resources, like iron ore.

The intrinsic value of an economy built on human resources, though, is that the supply is ever renewable and eternally springs forth, like most living matter, *under proper cultivation.*

The proper cultivation of human resources is based on two controllable factors: 1) national attitudes—the wholesome climate for growth; and 2) education—the nutrient that produces this "resource" in increasing abundance and ascending value.

One may totally disregard all social implications and consider only the economic factors involved and come rapidly to the conclusion that in nations where education is a "privilege" rather than a right, the nation suffers.

In some countries education is available only to the children of the rich. This is perilously close to being the case in the United States and Canada insofar as advanced education is concerned. Unless there is free and ready access to the highest quality of education, a false restriction is placed on the development of human resources. That is why even the most conservative and so–called right–wing economists favor free education through college and even graduate schools, for those who qualify scholastically.

Whole attitudes must change in America if it is to retain its leadership in human resources. There must be changes within the educational system itself and in the academic community, and changes in the attitudes of the laymen and the politicians.

First, we must rid ourselves of the inaccurate notion that education is a "privilege." It is no privilege; it is a

duty. We *must* have an increasingly educated population if we are to advance economically, philosophically
and socially. Our concern here is with the economic
future. Our technological advancement, our managerial advancement, our productive advancement, all depend not only on a rise in educational standards, but
also on the extension of education to greater numbers
of our citizens. We must increase our skills and broaden
our quest for knowledge, our ability to see logic, our
search for the elusive truths. If we do not do so, our
economic progress will be slowed.

Second, we must improve education. It must be im-
proved scientifically, by careful and expert study of
ends and means. Experimentation, such as New York
City's fiasco with political subdivisions of the central
educational system, can never help true education. Perhaps we are not encouraging creativity; perhaps, indeed, we have no way to measure it. Perhaps we are not
giving sufficient attention to gifted children; perhaps,
indeed, we fail to recognize and evaluate gifted children when we see them. Perhaps we fail in the methods
we employ in the teaching–learning process; perhaps,
indeed, we try to teach the wrong things. Perhaps—
perhaps: the one thing that is clear is that this is no
area for amateurs or self–styled experts.

It is possible that an uneducated person may become
a great manager in some area of management; it is
doubtful that he can become a great technologist, or
engineer, or scientist, or other important contributor to
the nation's economic progress. On the other hand, if
the uneducated manager had been educated, there is no
evidence to indicate that he would not have been an
even greater manager, a more important contributor to
the commonweal.

Thus it seems to boil down to this: If increased productivity increases *real* income; if an increase in *real*

income is one of the main deterrents to domestic inflation; then greater accessibility to education for all
Americans is one of the principal weapons against inflation in the future.

In another chapter we will show that taxation, far
from being a restraint on an "overheated" economy (a
term of the avant-garde thinkers among the Central
Planners), is more of a force to add to inflation. For the
present, let's consider taxation as it affects productivity.

One of the quickest ways to reduce productivity is to
discourage savings, investments, inventions, innova-
tions, risk–taking, capital formations, and technological improvements.

The greatest deterent to all of these is taxation. When
the government takes away part of the business incomes and personal incomes, it stifles what is broadly
called "incentives." Stifled are the incentives to save, to
invest, to innovate, to invent, to take financial risks and
form capital, to create new technologies—and, above
all, to work diligently.

In America we give up more than 30 per cent of our
income and profits to the tax collector.

Nearly 10 per cent of our population is engaged in
collecting taxes—pleasantly or unpleasantly—from
the other 90 per cent.

That preposterous creature, the "average man," a
cretin existing in the minds of intellectual snobs and
Madison Avenue panderers, works more than three
months out of every year for his governments—local,
state and federal—and in the near future will be working about four months a year, one–third of his time, for
them.

When historians analyze the unrest of the last two-
thirds of the twentieth century, they may find that
excessive taxation was a major culprit. It must be real-

ized, of course, that, except in wartime, taxation that is regarded as excessive results from unwise government spending.

Taxation has seriously affected productivity and therefore has restrained what otherwise might have been giant strides in advancement in the standard of living. The fact that in Canada and the United States productivity has increased during the periods of heaviest taxation does not imply that taxation *stimulates* productivity; quite the contrary, it indicates that the human resources are so great in those nations that productivity increased *despite* taxation. There is no way of knowing how much higher the living standards in the United States and Canada might be had it not been for the high tax demands.

In Britain, where taxes are also extremely high, the human resources were so restricted by labor laws, union rules, government regulations, and a generally abject attitude about work, that productivity actually declined; when the boost in taxes caused a cut in income, workers simply turned in less production, and a severe drop in *real* income resulted.

There were many other factors involved in Britain's monetary troubles of 1968, but taxes and productivity were paramount.

This situation led to a withdrawal of support by creditors, and a drop in capital expansion and capital investment. This fact, more than anything else, doomed Britain's economy, and its sole value is the lesson it should provide its neighbors in the Western world.

There are two vital and outstanding examples of differences in the way governments *react* to basic economic problems that should be taken more seriously by political leaders in the United States.

The first concerns taxation. In the early 1960s, West Germany was faced with a minor recession. Unemployment began to mount. Social leaders began to demand some action by the government. Instead of instituting some federal "make–work" projects, Chancellor Adenauer's government decided to cut taxes. This, it was explained, would cause more capital to flow into investment, which would cause greater expansion, which, in turn, would demand more manpower, thus restoring full employment. *Within two years the program was deemed an outstanding success.*

The second concerns unemployment in Canada. Shortly after the Liberal government of Prime Minister Pierre Elliott Trudeau was formed, consumer groups pressured for some kind of action to halt what was considered dangerous price inflation. The cost of living in Canada had moved up by 3 to 4 per cent in the 1967–68 period. (In the United States the increase was over 4 per cent in the same period.) At the same time, the Economic Council of Canada, a nonpartisan government advisory agency, reported that unemployment had increased by 4 per cent in one year to a rate of 5.1 per cent of the total work force. Canada's target is no more than a 3 per cent jobless rate.

Despite the national goals, the *Liberal* government of Canada decided to cut government spending to curb inflation.

In a policy statement that announced cancellation of numerous public works programs, including its traditional "winter program," the government specifically stated it would not spend Dominion funds to try to reduce the high rate of unemployment, because it believed that price stability was more important to the general economy.

Within two months after this announcement, the amount of capital investment in Canada had advanced significantly, after a lull of several months, and the jobless rate was beginning to drop and head toward its minimum 3 per cent "desired" level.

The lesson here is rather basic. When a capitalistic economy faces problems, it must cure them with capitalistic measures—that is, increase the flow of capital spending. This creates higher employment, higher national income, and increases the tax yield without boosting the tax rates. Capitalistic problems cannot be cured with socialistic remedies.

Only in a pure socialistic economy will socialistic measures, such as increased government spending and increased taxes, serve to relieve the problems. Experience indicates that even in socialistic societies, the device of government spending does not cure—it merely relieves the condition temporarily.

6. The Sky-riding
Chartlines

Without a single federal or state "program" to make work or stimulate spending, without any costly war to boost capital spending by government, without any artificial pump–priming whatsoever, the gross national product will reach a full *trillion* dollars, long before another decade has passed, and in the opinion of most economists, probably before 1975.

The GNP—the total value of the national output of goods and services, and the most accurate measure of our collective wealth—will reach one trillion, five hundred billion dollars before 1990 (probably by 1985), and when we enter the new century, it is estimated that it will reflect a total value of two and one–third trillion dollars.

For those who like to look at it in good, solid arabic numerals, it is: $2,334,000,000,000.

Divide that by the number of Americans and you have a theoretical—but inaccurate—per capita net worth for every American.

The fact remains that though the rich may become richer as the nation's gross national product advances, all who add to that gross national product, through the contribution of goods or services, will enjoy higher incomes and an advancing standard of living. For many, incomes will triple. The gains will be mostly in *real* income, based on advances in productivity, provided the government does not, in the interim, cheapen the money by paying vast amounts for unproductive services, either to ease the plight of nonproducers or to speed up the currency flow and pep up consumer spending.

The key, again, is productivity, and the greatest rewards will accrue to those who contribute to it.

An improvement in prosperity alone will affect savings and pensions to some extent. Prices tended to increase in good times, during recent years. Theoretically they shouldn't have, if productivity had kept pace with wage increases, but not since 1940 has productivity done that. A productivity gap has existed between consumer prices and output (which includes industrial production, agricultural items and services) since the end of World War II.

In modern society a higher level of income is customarily accompanied by higher prices. One reason for it is that, economically speaking, the cart is before the horse. Inflationary wage increases were granted on an almost universal basis during and after World War II at rates that generally outstripped any increases in productivity.

This caused general price increases in the whole consumer market during the next decade. The marked–up prices in turn goaded workers to seek even higher incomes to "catch up" with inflation—the inflation their previous raises had caused. When these increases were granted, prices, in time, resumed their climb.

It is doubtful that, in a free society dominated by publicly owned corporations and extremely strong trade and craft unions, there will ever be a genuine recognition of the full impact of industry-wide, nation-wide wage increases. One reason is that there is usually a lag between wide-scale wage boosts and resultant price increases. Sometimes this calm–before–the–storm lasts a year or more. It gives the recipient of the pay raise a false sense of prosperity, and he resents it when, later, higher prices erode his newly won economic advantage and reduce his effective buying power to the level that existed before he got his raise. Since he feels that he has been cheated by inflation, a nebulous force, the recipient goes after yet another raise. History shows that usually he has been successful.

Thus the pattern is repeated, causing what has come to be known as the "inflationary spiral."

This is the root cause of the inflation that has plagued the American economy since World War II. It, alone, would have been sufficient to cause a steady climb in consumer prices throughout the period. As a force, it has been aided enormously by government spending, which has provided a hefty inflationary wallop on its own, either by printing money to pay its mounting bills, or by borrowing from the commercial banks, thereby creating new bank deposits and greatly adding to the amount of money in circulation.

Since the end of World War II, the American economy has been subjected simultaneously to two kinds of inflationary pressures, one being described by the academic economists as "demand–pull inflation," the other as "seller–push inflation." One has been caused by the productivity gap, when wage and salary increases exceed and supersede the increases in productivity; the other has been caused by excessive government spending.

Increasingly, economists are finding agreement in the belief that a little bit of inflation may be good for us, and that it stimulates the economy and keeps things moving. Heretofore, a great many classical thinkers in the field believed that a little bit of inflation was like a little bit of pregnancy and that it had a predetermined course of growth. That no doubt would be true if all factors remained constant, but they do not. Recognizing this, the economic community, as a whole, is much more tolerant of inflationary forces than it was in the past.

It has been fairly well established that the American economy would not be seriously affected by the productivity gap alone, if it were not for the inflationary role played by government.

The increases granted to America's workers, in other words, would not alone cause intolerable inflationary pressures. It is only when the inflationary pressures caused by excessive government spending are added to the mild inflationary forces set in operation by union wage gains and agricultural price increases, that the chartlines soar skyward and the situation gets out of control.

The biggest obstacle, then, to further industrial wage increases and additional profits on agricultural products and further boosts in the rewards for performing services, is posed by government spending. Without excessive government spending, the economy apparently could withstand modest advances in the price levels without serious threat to the stability of the dollar.

The big enemy of the working man, therefore, seems to be the group of excessive spenders in government.

On the basis of this fact it would seem that organized labor would be in the forefront in demanding that government spenders practice restraint. Yet, incongruously, organized labor has been in the forefront in demanding ever larger government expenditures for domestic "social" projects. There are exceptions to this, of course. The International Brotherhood of Teamsters, largest trade union in the world, has been consistent in advocating a policy of restraint in federal spending. So has the International Typographical Union, and a few other craft unions. But other big ones—the Automobile Workers, the Steel Workers, the Electrical Workers, the Rubber Workers—maintain constant and consistent pressure on politicians at all levels to increase government outlays of cash on domestic projects.

If this seems shortsighted, union leaders will tell you that their concern is for the immediate future, the "next goal." Their consideration does not embrace the retired workers living on pensions. They are no longer dues–payers.

Between 1955 and fiscal 1968 (beginning July 1, 1967) Congress enacted more than 100 new federal programs, all nondefense in nature, all said to meet "domestic needs," and their total cost in the 1968 budget was a significant $16.5 billion. Sometimes we forget, in these days of huge figures and space age computers, that it takes one thousand million–dollar bills to equal one billion dollars. The "new projects" voted by government would require sixteen thousand five–hundred–million–dollar bills, if paid in that denomination.

This amount of money, if collected in single–dollar bills and laid end to end, would stretch out for 8,250,-000,000 feet, or 1,562,500 miles. Since the earth is 24,902 miles in circumference, this sum of money in single dollar bills laid end to end would wrap around the equator 62½ times.

In thousand–dollar bills laid end to end, it could form a lovely green center line on a highway stretching from New York to Minneapolis.

Essentially that's what is meant by the figure:

$$\$16,500,000,000.$$

It represents the total annual income of 5,500,000 Americans who earn the average of $3,000 per year.

That's how much the brand new domestic, non-defense projects enacted by the federal government between 1955 and 1968 cost American taxpayers in 1968: $165 annually to every man, woman and child, each one of the 200 million Americans; or the equivalent of a $227 annual raise to every employed person in the nation.

There is an unbroken pattern to show that new federal programs, once set up, continuously expand in scope and cost.

Administrative budget spending more than doubled from $64 billion in fiscal 1955 to $135 billion in 1968. Nondefense spending doubled, rising from less than $24 billion at the end of the Korean War to more than $49 billion. Strictly new nondefense programs accounted for more than half the increase; the remainder of the increase was due to both expansion of existing projects and rising costs of operation, which costs were prompted by the inflation that was caused by the projects themselves.

Government spending for nondefense programs is rapidly becoming an American way of life. A total of 112 new programs were adopted and set in motion between 1955 and 1968. The rate at which they are being created has accelerated—78 new ones since 1962; 46 of them between 1965 and 1968. Since 1962, an average of more than 12 new programs each year has been approved by Congress, compared with an annual average of four in the preceding six years.

The average initial cost of new programs launched since 1962 has been $430 million, compared with a starting cost of $100 million in the period from 1955 to 1962.

New programs enacted between 1962 and 1968 added $9 billion to the nondefense spending total in the 1968 budget—which plunged the nation into the deepest indebtedness in its history.

By mid–1968, $85 billion had been spent on the 112 new programs started since 1955. The American taxpayers have no measurement of the benefits accruing from such a titanic expenditure. No studies have been made to show how effective these programs have been.

There is no accountability.

Program by program, each one has increased tremendously. For instance, two examples are: the Food for Freedom program, which started in 1956 with an expenditure of $121 million, and in 1968 cost $1.8 billion; and the National Aeronautics and Space Agency, which was established in 1958 with an appropriation of $89 million, and cost $5.3 billion in 1968—after severe, painful and protested budgetary cuts.

In considering nondefense expenditures here, we are not taking into account the new programs and extensions of older programs financed through special trust funds set up by government. Such funds include the highway trust and the disability insurance trust, both established in 1956, and the trust fund for the Medicare program. Trust fund expenditures were $8.6 billion in 1955—they had grown to $44.5 billion in 1968.*

In the entire period under study, 1955–1968, only one federal nondefense program was terminated. It was

*Report, Tax Foundation, Inc., September 16, 1967.

the accelerated public works program started in 1963. All possible savings were wiped out when every function of that program was incorporated in other programs providing the same kinds of public facilities.

There was a drop in expenditures in only one project —but that, too, was offset when the same functions were incorporated, at higher expense and cost, in other programs.

It is necessary to look at the immediate past in this manner if we are to consider the impact of inflation in the future.

During the period under study the cost of living had moved upward month by month at a rather steady pace, averaging 3 per cent or higher.

Based on past experience we must expect two basic inflationary thrusts to continue into the foreseeable future:

1. Government will continue to spend excessively.

2. Workers, both organized and unorganized, will seek and receive compensation boosts in excess of an increase in productivity.

These two forces will cause further price inflation in the future, and force more depreciation of the dollar.

Will the United States face hyperinflation—runaway inflation, where the price level increases a hundred times or more? This, say the experts, is highly unlikely. Hyperinflation is associated with inadequate tax systems, or crushing defeats in major wars, or inept governments, or irresponsible people who have not learned the necessary restraints of self–government.

These are the conditions that induce governments to run the money printing presses, either in desperation or because of irresponsibility at high levels.

Critical though we may be of the American economic experiment, such conditions are not likely to exist in the United States. Though Americans may not have fully mastered the difficult art of self-government, they exercise a greater measure of restraint in spending than those in many other civilized self–governing countries, such as Britain and France.

What it boils down to is not how much a government spends, but what effect its spending will have on the economy. Americans have been concerned—perhaps quite properly—with causes rather than effects. The day is nigh when public officials must alter their perspectives to see what conditions result in the economy when they spend for "programs" that are deemed necessary.

There is no gain whatsoever if the government sets up a program to raise the standard of living of one group in the economic community and in so doing sets off an inflationary spiral that depresses the standard of living of all those on pensions and fixed incomes. To the contrary, this is likely to inspire the government to start up an additional inflationary program seeking to help those with fixed incomes who have been hurt. It becomes a relentless, never–ending race against rising costs. A dog chasing his own tail has precisely as much direction and purpose—and beneficial reward.

The outlook for Americans more accurately is for what has come to be known as creeping inflation— about the same as we have experienced since the end of World War II.

This is due to the mutual incompatibility of what Dr. John P. Wernette, professor of Business Administration at the University of Michigan, describes as the "Three F's," which constitute three separate national goals. The three F's are: *full employment, freedom,* and *flation.*

To explain:

Full employment has come to be a term standing for prosperity—a high level of employment, a low level of unemployment, and generous earnings at all levels.

Freedom in this particular relates to the corporate and commercial world—the freedom of workers to organize, the freedom of managements and unions to engage in collective bargaining without accountability to the public or the government, the freedom of the managements to set prices on the basis of operational costs, including labor costs.*

Flation is something that exists in the absence of *in*flation and *de*flation and reflects a horizontal level of commodity prices.

The incompatibility of the three F's is readily apparent. It can be reasoned that any two of these goals can be easy to obtain, but not all three, that is:

· Freedom and Flation (No Full Employment)
· Full Employment and Flation (No Freedom to bargain)
· Full Employment and Freedom (No Flation)

While the federal government is committed to aspire to all three goals, in actual practice it is active in behalf of but two of them—full employment and freedom—and it vitiates flation because it realizes that if you have the other two, you cannot have a horizontal price line, or flation.

The government is pledged to try to maintain full employment and to avoid business slumps that might result in lower corporate profits and higher unemployment.

As a result, economic machinery has been in existence since 1947 and maintained on a standby emergency basis, like an ambulance or a fire truck, to go into operation with "stimulants" whenever a business downturn looms. This is provided under the Full Employment Act, which created the President's Council of

---

*Excepted are such general regulations as antitrust controls and the supervision of public utilities.

Economic Advisers, a group of experts charged with responsibility for scanning the business horizons and warning the President of the appearance of any ill winds that might send business barometers tumbling.

As a result, prices have no time to fall; stimulants are applied and under each recovery program prices are pushed up a bit.

The unlearned lesson is this: *government action rarely allows prices to decline, but usually pushes prices higher.*

Most thoughtful Americans would zealously guard the freedom of organized labor to bargain to the best of its ability under the broad restrictions now set forth in law. Embodied in that right, however, is the privilege of securing wage increases in excess of productivity increases at times when business is good and employment is at a high level. This raises labor cost per unit of output (since the unchanged rate of productivity results in the same number of units being produced at a higher labor cost) and this, in turn, prods the employers to post higher prices on whatever it is that labor is producing. This results in the classical "seller–push inflation." Employers are not reluctant to raise prices, because business is good and demand is running high; hence they're not too unwilling to grant the wage increases.

Looking at the situation candidly and realizing that the nation will be subjected to continuing inflation, it is necessary to assess the impact of inflation on the whole economy. What harm, in other words, will a *little* inflation cause?

Experts are in general agreement on inflation's effects on the economy. They include the charges that inflation:

· Robs some persons of their savings and pensions and gives unearned gains to others.

· Discourages savings and thrift, thereby reducing investment capital.

· By decreasing the supply of investment capital, retards growth.

· Is detrimental to production, for it makes the processes more costly.

· Encourages speculation vis–à–vis investment.

· Hampers managerial decision–making, by making future costs unpredictable.

· Discourages efficiency, both at the commercial–industrial level, and among individuals.

· Induces waste by cheapening the value of everything.

· Picks up speed and impetus, if only because people buy and hoard in anticipation of higher prices.

· Leads ultimately to the classical economic hang–up that results in "boom and bust."

The conditions listed in the foregoing result, the experts say, from a *little* inflation, which does not give productivity a chance to catch up with prices, or prices a chance to back down to productive rates.

This represents the most accurate picture of what lies ahead for America unless government spending can be vastly curtailed and the salary–wage scales can be leveled off for a considerable stretch of time.

Most Americans are unwilling to freeze salaries and wages. It is opposed to the national policy and the American conscience.

Viewing government operations honestly, it must also be admitted that there is slim likelihood that the enormous spending programs will be cut back to any appreciable degree.

For the average American it seems to boil down to this: If you can't lick inflation, and you can't join it— learn to live with it.

But how to live with it—that is the big question.

7. Profit By
Going Into Debt

The full force of inflation finally made itself felt in the United States in 1968. It wasn't until all of the figures were reported and calculated in the spring of 1969, however, that there was official confirmation of what every breadwinner had been suspecting right along—that the increase in the cost of living in 1968 wiped out in its entirety every increase in income during the same period.

Incomes in 1968 rose 5 per cent. The cost of living in 1968 rose by a bit more than 5 per cent.

The preponderance of wage increases and salary boosts had been given either for "merit" or as a result of labor contracts that had been signed a year or two earlier. The increments, in other words, were not the result of an increase in productivity. Thus the family head whose paycheck was sweetened from $150.00 weekly to $157.50—a 5 per cent increase—didn't gain a penny.

What was grossly unfair about it, though, was that

the man who did increase his productivity, who actually earned a boost of 5 per cent, found he had contributed his sweat, or brainpower, or energy, or time, for nothing. His increase in productivity gained him nothing; in fact, it helped to contribute to inflation by making the product of his labors, either in goods or services, available in *greater* abundance—at *higher* prices.

As a result of his 1968 experience, he will be a hard man to convince that an increase in productivity offsets inflationary increases in wages or salaries.

Herein is exposed a great gray area of economic thinking that requires further academic exploration. It has been regarded as axiomatic not only that an increase in productivity merits an increase in rewards for the producer, but that those rewards, backed by the added productivity, are noninflationary.

Obviously this is untrue unless the productivity boost is universal or the commensurate increases in compensation are confined solely to those who have contributed to added productivity.

Moreover, an increase in the output of goods and services that carry higher price tickets compounds the inflationary impact, rather than lessens it, thus leaving another classical axiomatic theory of economics in doubt: the theory that an increase in output results in a lowering of prices on the goods or services thus found in greater abundance. It is not generally true in modern economic experience, because general price increases are simply added to the greater supply of goods or services.

There's a side effect, too, that must be correlated with the increase in output. It, too, has been ignored in the past in arriving at the economic philosophy and "axioms" that have guided thinking. When a corporation enjoys an increase in productivity in times of prosperity it is reflected in both profits and capacity, and may very likely result in an increase in the value of its securities. This, in turn, raises the limit on the corporation's ability to borrow money from the banks. Since a wisely managed corporation borrows to the extent of its credit, this further depletes the money supply, and results in yet more inflationary pressures.

A rather strong case can be made, it seems, to show that productivity increases, unless they are almost universal, are not at all anti–inflationary but rather are strongly inflationary, when general wage and income levels are increased.

In recent years wages and salaries (general income) have been increased from 2 to 5 per cent annually with great consistency.

Another facet of the American economy that is begging for further exploration and study manifested itself to some degree in the great inflationary burst of 1968. That is the impact on the economy of the spending by and for young people who, generally, are nonproductive for one reason or another, and because of their nonproductivity constitute a solid inflationary spending bloc.

Americans under twenty–five years of age constituted nearly half of the population of the United States in 1969 and will outnumber all other Americans by 1971. It is estimated that in 1969 these young people accounted directly for about one-third of the spending by individuals. When you add the amounts spent in their behalf by their elders, their particular "market" approached 50 per cent of all the money that was spent that year by individuals.

Since a large proportion of those under twenty–five are in school and up to certain ages in many states are prohibited by law from working, these are nonproductive spenders and, as such, constitute a major inflationary force. This is a relatively new spending force in America and has not heretofore been calculated into the economic analyses.

It's time it was.

These kids are even freer spenders than members of the generation immediately preceding them, and that generation set all-time records in improvidence.

Both the youngest generation (those under twenty–five) and the generation immediately preceding it are the most thriftless in recorded economic history, if one discounts the forced savings accumulated in life insurance policies. Insurance companies have really sold thrift in America and enough salesmen have wedged their feet into a sufficient number of doors to create a great bulwark of savings. It is true, also, that the savings accounts in the nation's thrift institutions tower at all-time peaks, except when money gets tight or taxes are due or the stock market drops and exposes some good bargains.

Discounting the inflationary factor from the total volume of savings reduces the figure considerably, of course. But analysis of the individual accounts in the thrift institutions is both revealing and frightening.

Increasingly, year by year, the savings accounts are reaching toward the maximum figure allowed for individuals under the insurance programs of the Federal Deposit Insurance Corporation. In mutual savings banks this is $25,000 for individuals and $50,000 for joint accounts. The number of large savings accounts increases each year, and analysis of the ownership of these accounts shows that they are in older age brackets though not necessarily in the higher income brackets.

Further analyses show that with each passing year the smaller accounts are owned by fewer and fewer young people (under twenty–five).

In short, there's more money in the savings banks, but it's not owned by the young.

The improvident predecessors in the economic arena did not teach the young the habits of thrift. Perhaps they will acquire the habit as they mature; perhaps not. Meanwhile, their unexplored and undocumented attitudes toward money, income, spending and prudence have great bearing on the economy, and on inflation, and hence, on the welfare and well-being of all other Americans, in every age group.

There's more to the foregoing statement than meets the eye.

The security, the happiness, the ability to stay out of debt, the retirement years of every American now living may depend in great measure on the soundness of the economic judgment of youth of twenty–one and younger!

The fellow in his late thirties or forties who believes he has a comfortable nest egg tucked away may have learned a lesson when in 1968 his savings account paid him exactly zero in interest because the dividend of 5 per cent was wiped out by a greater than 5 per cent increase in living costs; but he may be in for a horrible jolt when he learns that the increase in living costs was double the amount his savings earned in interest in any one year. He may face a hideous truth when he learns, upon analysis, that hordes of young people, who outnumber him two to one, hold the answer as to whether or not his savings, the product of his years of thrift, will be permitted to grow, or will be wiped out entirely!

Common sense indicates that an educational program in both thrift and economics is urgently needed.

Such a course of instruction might be difficult to set up, though, for want of qualified instructors. The truth is that although most people handle money throughout their lives, few know its true value or understand how to preserve its worth, if only because they haven't been able to figure out how to cope with inflation.

By this time, of course, nearly everyone understands what inflation *does*—that as prices go up the value of your money goes down in direct proportion. They realize that yesterday's $75 suit costs $125 today; that the $2,500 car of 1950 costs over $4,000 today; that a first-class $18 tire now costs $40; that the $3 office call at the doctor's now takes $8 or $10; that the 3¢ newspaper is now a dime, or more.

The effect of inflation is easy to gauge. What is more elusive is figuring out how to halt it. What is even more challenging is how to manage your own affairs to compensate for it and to prevent, as much as possible, the impact of the loss on your purchasing power.

People who work hard for their money and take a long time to accumulate it naturally feel cheated when the declining value of the inflated dollar robs them of their purchasing power. The purists among the savers —those who mistrust and eschew the use of credit— have hardly been able to save fast enough, for instance, to keep up with rising real estate prices in recent years and to plan on paying cash for a home.

A home that cost $20,000 in 1945 gained in value at the rate of $1,000 a year in most metropolitan areas, making it worth $40,000 in 1965, and $45,000 in 1970. In many localities the increase has been greater.

On the surface this sounds as though it may be all right if you are selling, but not so good if you're buying. The fellow who bought his house in 1945 for $20,000 and figures to make a handsome profit by selling it for $45,-000 in today's market will find that he's dealing with profitless profit, for he'll have to turn right around and spend $45,000 for another home to live in, no better than the one he's selling. The owner's value in the inflated price on his home can be realized only by hanging onto his property. It becomes, then, an asset worth $45,000 for which he paid only $20,000. The enhancement in price by $25,000 is of value to the owner only as collateral against which he may borrow. But his loan will be made in inflated dollars, and he'll repay it with inflated dollars. In this way, and only in this way, can the fortunate owner of a $45,000 home for which he paid $20,000 "beat" inflation.

If the inflationary spiral continues through the years in which he is repaying his loan, the bank or the lender suffers the loss of the dollar's value.

Let's say the home owner borrows $10,000 for a period of three years at interest of 7 per cent per annum. If the cost of living rises by 5 per cent each year, the dollars he pays back are worth 5 per cent less each year. Since they cost him 7 per cent to borrow when they were worth 5 per cent more, his actual borrowing cost is 2 per cent.

He might not see it quite like that in his account books, but technically, that's how he fares.

But he has to hold onto his property to get the goodies.

Going into debt, then, is one way to keep abreast of the effects of inflation. This is exactly the opposite of the basic rules of prudence laid down by economic philosophers from Adam Smith to Ben Franklin to the worried fathers of a generation ago. Their advice was: Stay out of debt as much as possible. "Neither a borrower nor a lender be," said Shakespeare, and this advice has been stated and restated in one way or another through the ages.

In some circumstances in today's inflated economy, wise borrowing is the epitome of prudence.

The man who went into debt by taking out a twenty-year mortgage and buying his $20,000 home in 1945, learned in 1965, when his mortgage was paid, that his property was worth $40,000, and therefore counted himself lucky. He may not have considered the fact that the dollars he repaid to the bank each year had a steadily declining value that constituted a purchasing power loss to the bank and a purchasing power gain to him. Without considering the interest, he had to repay $1,000 per year. The $1,000 he repaid in 1965, twenty years after borrowing it, was worth only a bit more than $500 in 1945 dollars. Actually, to maintain a constant purchasing value of the currency, he should have repaid the bank something close to $2,000 that final year, and only slightly less than that in 1964, and so on.

Thus he gained in two ways—the value of his house doubled, but the money he used to buy it retained a constant value in the face of inflation that, in effect, *increased* his purchasing power of that particular item, with each passing year.

In theory, each $1,000 that he repaid to the bank was to have purchased him $1,000 worth of house. He would repay $20,000 and own $20,000 worth of property.

Instead, each $1,000 that he repaid bought him $1,000 worth of house plus 5 per cent, each year, so that at the end of twenty years each $1,000 that had been repaid to the bank bought him $2,000 worth of house, for a total of $40,000.

Contrast the experience of this man with that of the fellow who had been brought up to believe in all of the old virtues of thrift and who, being opposed to borrowing money from a bank, even on a mortgage, decided to save his money and pay cash for his house.

If he started in 1945 and decided he'd save $1,000 a year for twenty years, planning to buy his $20,000 house in 1965, he would never have made it.

If he realized in 1950 that his $20,000 house was then selling for $25,000, he would also have recognized the fact that the $5,000 he had saved was insufficient and that there remained only fifteen years in which to save

$20,000. Therefore, sticking to his planned prudence, he would start saving at the rate of $1,335 per year toward his dream house.

Imagine his surprise in 1955 when he learned that his house was then worth $30,000, and that in ten years—half his allotted time—he had saved only $11,675. He'd have to revise his figures again, and on the basis that he'd have to save $18,325 within the next ten years, plan to save $1,833 per year in order to have enough cash to buy his elusive dream house.

Taking stock again in 1960, he discovered that the house was then worth $35,000 and that with only five years left to his savings program, he had saved only $20,840! In the next five years he'd have to save $14,160, or at the rate of $2,832 per year!

Suppose that even then, after fifteen years of frustration, our methodical saver had not learned his lesson and went ahead with a belt–tightening program to save $2,832 per year for the next five years.

By 1965, at the end of the twenty years, he would have saved $35,000 with which to buy his house—which then was available only for $40,000.

After twenty years of systematic thrift, he was still $5,000 short of his goal. He had saved $15,000 more than he had intended to, and it was only 75 per cent of what he should have saved.

"How *do* those Joneses do it?" his wife asked as they drove past the $40,000 home of the man who twenty years earlier had gone ahead with a mortgage.

"Aw, Jones has no brains—he's in debt up to his ears," said her husband, as he headed their ancient car back to their tiny rented apartment.

The foregoing is, of course, a harsh illustration to point up the wisdom of programmed indebtedness as a hedge against inflation. The saver would have garnered some interest along the way, which is not calculated in our figures credited to his account, and chances are he could have swung the deal at the end of his twenty–year saving stint. A saver of that stature could have sold the string he had been saving to make up the difference!

Please note the reference to *programmed* indebtedness. Debt is a two–edged blade and while it can help cut through the balloons of inflation in the hands of the skilled and thoughtful user, it can also inflict severe wounds on the careless.

The foregoing account points out the essential role played by the banks in helping individuals to combat inflation.

It also points out the need for broader supervision of the credit–policing and credit–reporting agencies, for surely the man who borrowed to the hilt in 1945 was a wiser man than the one who had saved $1,000 that year toward his dream house.

Yet, any credit report would have shown the saver to be the better risk.

8. It'll Never Be
the Same Again

There's a chain of clothing stores that has a marvelous singing commercial: "Where the values go up, up, up, and the prices go down, down, down." No doubt this is true of that clothing store, but for most of the things you buy, the exact opposite is true. The *prices* go up, up, up while the value goes down, down, down. A darker side of inflation is the reduction in quantity and of quality as a compromise to the imposition of even larger price increases.

The classic example in America is the 5–cent candy bar. While the price has gone to 10 cents, the size of the average candy bar has been halved from 2½ ounces to 1¼ ounces. The increased price plus the reduced size represents a 400 per cent increase in the cost of the candy, but in addition, some manufacturers have made substitutions in the ingredients, using less expensive goodies to tease and please the palates of customers. The final effect is what probably amounts to a 500 per cent increase in the cost of a candy bar, over a span of but two decades.

The pricing of candy bars will neither disrupt the economy nor jeopardize the average family budget, but the truth is, this semiluxury item, the candy bar, is representative of a great many other items that are basically essential to either survival or well-being. Even where the candy bar is concerned, however, the worker who was accustomed to having a wholesome 2½–ounce 5–cent bar in his lunch box as dessert, now must buy two 1¼–ounce 10–cent bars to get the same amount of belly–pleasing bulk. Twenty cents today buys him the same *quantity* that a nickel once did.

Even after paying a 400 per cent increase in the cost of his lunch pail dessert, he may be shortchanged as to *quality*.

An added penalty of inflation is the fact that in some cases, possibly nowhere can he buy the same *quality* product that he used to buy, no matter how much he is willing to pay. Because of inflated *costs*, producers may deem it impractical or imprudent or unfeasible to manufacture a product with the highest–quality ingredients.

Isn't this true of baker's bread that you buy in your supermarket or grocery store?

It's true of a great many things. Have you tried to buy a high–grade woolen suit made of long–staple fibers? It's nonexistent. Have you tried to buy all–leather shoes of the finest calfskin? Unless they're custom–made, they, too, are nonexistent. How about prepared meat? Have you tried to buy genuine hickory–smoked, non-salted, nonprocessed bacon? None is to be found any-where, unless you know a farmer with gourmet tastes who is doing his own thing with his porkers and will spare you a side of bacon.

The point is, the amount of money you are willing to

spend may avail you nothing insofar as certain items are concerned, for they will have been eliminated from the scene by inflation.

The unique American distribution system that has done so much for the American consumer, is, itself, falling prey to the ravages of inflation.

Merchandising experts frequently predetermine a price range for a product, particularly an item of food, declaring that the biggest consumer response will be at such and such a price level, thus placing a burden on all participants in the distributive process to meet that price range. Under such circumstances, it is not uncommon to sacrifice quality in favor of a price that reflects less than the total amount of inflation. A compromise is struck; a can of soup that might have normally increased in price by 10 cents, is cheapened in quality by 5 cents per can, and increased in price by 5 cents.

How to spot this? The clue is frequently to be found in items that are restricted to packaging of fixed sizes. Cans, bottles and some cardboard cartons are in "fixed" sizes that are not only well established with the consumer, but are standardized throughout the industry, with the result that the canning, bottling or cardboard–folding machines are standardized. Because it costs a company so much to reduce the *quantity* of its product and put it into a smaller container, it is tempted to reduce the *quality.* Quite often this becomes a compromised factor: the quality is reduced slightly and the price is increased slightly.

The consumer must be on the alert for this device in any item where ingredients are blended together, be it soup, cereal, fabric, furniture, furnishings, building materials, automobiles, or even television sets. In this age of standardized mass distribution, the substitution of ingredients is common practice, and the determination of quality is increasingly difficult.

There's an adverse side effect of the modern distribution system that relates somewhat to the problem of inflation, but is more directly concerned with the matter of quality. It involves fresh produce, fresh fish and, in some respects, fresh meats in the grocery or supermarket.

Your food retailer, the manager of the supermarket that you patronize, or the manager or owner of the grocery store that you favor, endeavors to supply you with "fresh" produce (basically vegetables and fruits) throughout the year, irrespective of the season. To do so, he must negotiate with a wholesaler–distributor (a distributor who sells to the retailer) and agree to take certain quantities of specific fruits or vegetables throughout the year. The wholesaler-distributor, in turn, has to negotiate with a commodity dealer, and has to agree to buy certain quantities of specific items throughout the year.

The desired effect and goal of this system are the stabilization of prices throughout the year, keeping them in a narrow range (that is, apples in March cost only a few cents more per pound than do apples in October when they are being harvested in quantity). From a nutritional point of view, also, this eliminates the "seasonal" glut of foodstuffs in the stores, and provides almost all foods, fresh, on a year–round basis no matter where you might live. In Caribou, Maine, or International Falls, Montana, or Bismark, North Dakota, anyone can buy "fresh" tomatoes in January—or cucumbers, or grapes, or squash, or celery, or avocadoes.

Quite simply, the man who contracts to supply tomatoes twelve months a year has to arrange to have tomatoes ripening twelve months a year, and he does this on large scale in fields ranging from the Imperial

Valley in California to Texas and Arizona, the Gulf States, Northern Florida, and northward with the advance of the spring season.

In August, however, when "native" tomatoes are at their peak in all of the Northern states from Maine to Oregon and Washington, the largest retailers in all communities will be offering tomatoes from the great growing fields of Delaware, Maryland and Southern New Jersey or California's fertile Imperial Valley.

A grocer in Massachusetts, within short trucking distance of many acres of vine–ripening native tomatoes, will be selling tomatoes trucked in from New Jersey. If he wants to sell tomatoes in January or even in July, a few weeks before the local varieties ripen, he has to take what his supplier offers him at the time that native produce is ready for the shelves.

He may carry both kinds in stock. It's up to the shopper to distinguish between the mass–distributed, ripened-en-route variety, and the kind that is called "native," and is most likely vine–ripened. Quite often there is very little difference in price.

More remarkable is the fact that there's so little difference in the price of tomatoes bought in January and those bought in August, though for the customer of that Massachusetts store, January's tomatoes may be shipped three thousand miles, and August's may have traveled only a couple of hundred miles.

Even more remarkable is the fact that the supermarket in Camden, New Jersey, in the heart of the July–August tomato country, has to price its tomatoes about the same as those in Massachusetts—or Michigan or North Dakota.

Involved in this is an intricate commodity price structure that interrelates rail freight rates with trucking rates, and that seeks to apportion the shipping costs among all consumers on a stabilized year–round basis.

An increase in costs anywhere along the line—a wage boost for pickers or for railroad workers or truckers, or the higher cost of fertilizers, or of shipping cartons, or even of highway tolls—can affect prices throughout the nation simultaneously, at any season of the year.

The point I've been trying to make in the preceding few pages is that you shouldn't be fooled by those who ask you cynically, "It's only *money*, isn't it?"

No, it isn't.

It's tomatoes in season.

It's almond–*flavored* candy, instead of *real* almonds. It's a lunch pail that doesn't offer quite the same quality of lunch that it used to.

Money is regarded as a tangible thing, by most people —as tangible as real estate or a car or a pool table.

It really isn't, though. It's as tangible as a suit of clothes or a dress that may lose value with changing styles.

Without getting too elementary about it, while money is a physical, tangible thing that you can see, hold, feel, even taste, its value is relative. It changes.

In recent years—since World War II—money has had a depreciation value, like automobiles. It has come to be almost as predictable in its depreciation as is your car.

You know that if you buy a new car this year, it will be worth no more than the "blue book" allows for it when you go to trade it in two years from now. If it's to be valued at $1,000 less than you paid for it, you figure this to be a *cost* of owning your car, along with gas, oil, equipment, repairs, taxes, interest, insurance and garaging.

Similarly, you must realize, from the experience in the last half–dozen years, that the dollars you earn this year will be worth anywhere from 3 per cent to 5 per cent less next year when you trade them in for whatever they will buy.

You know, by making comparisons, that the dollars you use today are worth only 50 cents when compared with the dollars that were used fifteen, twenty or twenty-five years ago.

As a prudent user of dollars, you should recognize the fact that the erosion process in the dollar's value goes on all the time, week in and week out, year in, year out.

It *costs* you money to own money, just as it *costs* you money (depreciation) to own your car. This is true of money whether you use it or not, just as it's true of your car whether you drive it or not. While nestling in your pocket, money loses some of its worth.

You accept the depreciation of your car as an inevitable consequence of progress and model changes. You adjust your budgeting accordingly.

If you were to use your car to produce some income, say, in an amount greater than the $500 per year you calculate to lose to depreciation, you would thereby reduce the *cost* of owning the car.

If you accept the fact that, like your car, your money costs you money simply to own it, then you will accept the burden of trying to reduce that cost.

Currently it costs just about 5 per cent per year to own money. The dollar you earn in January is worth 95 cents in December.

Put in a savings account that pays 5 per cent per annum, your money has worked for you to produce an amount equal to the loss to depreciation (or inflation).

In the meantime, though, you have to spend much of your money. You have to buy food, clothing, shelter, transportation, medical and dental care and myriad goods and services that you need or want simply to live. No one these days saves all that he earns.

If you can save 10 per cent of your income and collect

5 per cent interest on it, you're still suffering the depreciation–inflation loss on 90 per cent of what you earn.

The trouble is, you don't notice what's happening to your dollars the way you notice what's happening to the value of your car. Most breadwinners are too busy "bringing home the bacon," or "hustling the buck," to pay much heed to the silent cost of owning money.

Moreover, household budgets are notoriously inexact. Not only do costs keep changing, needs keep varying and conditions keep fluctuating, the plain truth is that most families never know their net worth, anyway. The nearest they come to an accounting is when they do their exercises for Form 1040 and the tax man.

Over a span of time it is possible for the average family to measure the cost of inflation. Over the dozen years between 1958 and 1970, many people witnessed the price of a loaf of bread climb from 19 cents to 30 cents; steak increase from $1.04 per pound to $1.40; milk jump from 22 cents a quart to 31 cents.

Families don't stop to think that the dollar that was worth 100 pennies in 1939 is worth just about 40 pennies today; that in thirty years the dollar has lost 60 per cent of its value in purchasing power—or any kind of power.

This doesn't mean that the cost of living has increased by 60 per cent.

It has increased, in thirty years, by 250 per cent!

Our problem—and it's national in scope—is that we have come to evaluate the effect of inflation on a year-to-year basis. We figure we're lucky or unlucky in any given year by the amount of the hike in the cost of living.

An absolutely stable average price level, while highly desired, is thought to be unattainable in today's world. Therefore we *accept*, without reaction, some sort of annual price increase.

It boils down to something like this:

When prices rise 1 to 2 per cent per year we have what is known as "creeping inflation," and it is said to be something that the country as a whole can live with comfortably. It is not thought to cause wide-scale undue hardships.

If prices reach a 3 or 4 per cent increase per year as in 1967 and 1968, or 5 per cent as in 1969, the economists say we have "galloping" inflation and they try to do something about it.

Both politically and economically, we place almost total reliance on the Federal Reserve Board to curb inflation when it reaches the "galloping" stage.

Totally ignored is the fact that once the Federal Reserve swings into action in its many ways, all of them calculated to clamp down on credit and to increase the cost of borrowing money, great damage has already been done. We do not ever turn the tables around and indulge in some "deflation." We cannot. This would mean unemployment, loss of jobs, loss of income, pay cuts, and the like, none of which would be permitted by voters in today's volatile society.

What happens is a temporary lull in the pressure of inflation, a leveling–off, which permits the economy to cool a bit and adjust to the 4 or 5 per cent price increase that has already been realized. The new price level is thus absorbed into the pricing structure.

The precipitous acts of the Federal Reserve Board during the last several years, while doing nothing to roll back price levels, have imposed arbitrary and unjust hardships on the unsuspecting and the uninvolved.

Those among us, both individuals and businesses, who have already borrowed to the hilt to take advantage of the price rises, are much better off than those who have waited, only to find that the Federal Reserve has raised the discount rate or increased the required reserves of banks, or lowered the amount of margin allowable in the purchase of securities. Those who have waited find it much more difficult to get credit, and much costlier, if they succeed.

It has become a sort of game during recent years with sophisticated businesses and sophisticated individuals to keep "borrowed up" as much of the time as possible, to beat the rising cost of renting money, which is the Federal Reserve Board's only tool for fighting inflation.

In toto, it is an ineffective weapon. For one thing, its main purpose is to increase the cost of doing business, thereby, it is said, inhibiting growth and slowing expansion. Although growth and expansion are supposed to cause the production of more goods and make available more services, thus reducing the upward pressure to increase prices, somehow, in modern economic reasoning, growth and expansion are believed to be inflationary, simply because they cause fuller employment.

In practice, however, the most pronounced effect of the Federal Reserve's credit–tightening has been the posting of higher prices all along the line, to compensate for the increased cost of doing business that has been caused by restricting credit and making it costlier.

It's really not anti–inflationary.

From our observations in earlier chapters we have determined that inflation results basically from three sources:

1. Excessive expansion of the money supply, usually resulting from too much government spending.

2. Wage increases that exceed, in total, the productivity increases of all workers.

3. Pricing practices of some companies that reflect unreasonable markups for the purpose of producing unusually high profits.

What, then, are the "cures" for inflation?

Can government reduce its spending? It tries. Congress inveighs. In the end, though, congressmen cannot agree among themselves on what is to be cut from government budgets, and, generally, no two editorialists can see eye to eye on what should be trimmed from the expenditures, with the result that promises of spending cuts remain just that—promises. The modest budget cuts that do come from weeks of wrangling are accompanied by tax increases, either temporary or hidden— the government's contribution to the fight against inflation.

It must not be forgotten that inflation hits the government just as severely as it does the consumer in Dayton, Ohio, or anywhere else—and the government of the United States is the biggest single consumer in the world!

A great many government expenditures cannot be trimmed by so much as a dime, for they are fixed by law. These include interest on the ever–increasing debt, veterans' benefits, and other payouts that are unalterable obligations.

One great saving that could change the entire economic picture, insofar as government spending is concerned, would be the end of the Vietnam war. The elimination of the need to spend billions for that program would not only eliminate the current inflationary pressures, but also permit, without causing any inflation, the expenditure of greater amounts on domestic programs, such as relief for distressed urban areas of the nation.

This accounts for the fact that a great many conservative economic thinkers have joined with liberals in urging a speedy end to the nation's commitments in Vietnam.

As a philosophical sidelight, it is interesting to think that the Vietnam war has produced one domestic benefit in that it has caused conservative economists to share common economic goals with the so-called left-wing or ultraliberal economic philosophers.

At any rate, it's unlikely that relief can come from great cuts in government spending.

It is equally unlikely that wages can be controlled.

It is illogical to believe that corporate prices can be controlled unless wages are controlled.

This, then, places the whole burden of controlling the inflation on the Federal Reserve Board, a virtual Supreme Court of finance.

The Federal Reserve Board is charged with one major chore—the obligation to keep the U.S. economy on an even keel.

The "Fed," as it is called by the bankers, controls the supply of money available to the total economy. When business is slow and spenders are cautious, the Fed makes more money available to the banks and thus makes it easier for consumers to borrow money. When inflation is a threat, it makes less money available to the banks, thus making it more difficult for the consumers to borrow—and to spend.

The net result of a highly complicated process is really as simple as all that—more money in supply when times are slow; less money when the economy is heated up dangerously.

The three main tools used by the Fed in regulating the supply of money are these:

1. It makes changes in the percentage of money that banks are required to maintain in reserve to back up their deposits. If the "required reserve" is 20 per cent, for instance, a bank must keep in reserve $1.00 for every $5.00 it has in deposits.

2. It makes changes in the "discount rate," which, quite simply, is the rate of interest that the Fed charges to its member banks that borrow money from it.

3. It makes decisions in its "Open Market Operations" on the support or lack of support of government bonds. Through this function it either frees or freezes huge amounts of money that affect the total economy.

Considering these functions in order, here's what the Federal Reserve Board can do to control the economy:

1. It can raise the reserve requirement, forcing banks to keep larger sums in reserve, and making less money available for lending to customers.

2. It can raise the discount rate, making it costlier for banks to borrow from the central bank, which in turn causes local banks to boost their interest rates to borrowers, thus discouraging credit activity on the part of both the borrower and the lender.

3. It can sell, rather than buy, government bonds in the open market, and by causing "bargains" in the market, force banks to buy the securities, thus decreasing their reserves and reducing their lending power.

In the absence of special legislation, such as the wage and price controls voted in wartime, this Federal Reserve function constitutes the nation's total arsenal against inflation.

Each weapon in that arsenal is directed against credit.

Individual credit, as we have shown in preceding chapters, is an unscientific, unpoliced, nebulous factor.

That's why inflation does not hit all consumers equally.

Some may borrow liberally, to counteract the ravages of dollar depreciation.

Some may be prohibited from doing so, and thus be subjected to a brutal cut in purchasing power, an actual income cut, caused by inflation.

The Federal Reserve has weapons that fire broadly at the whole economy, blasting away at round numbers—

but the shrapnel from the exploding shells that it fires strikes mostly at the poor, those with lowly credit ratings.

These are the real victims of inflation.

9. The Two Weapons

For Individuals

There is no way for an individual to alleviate or relieve the effects of inflation on his income. If what he earns buys less than he intended it should, he has been robbed, purely and simply, and there's no way to get that money back. A 5 per cent increase in the cost of living in any one year (as in 1968, for example) means, incontrovertibly, a 5 per cent reduction in the effective income of every individual breadwinner.

There are some whose thrift, good fortune or cleverness has provided them with investable assets that equal or exceed the equivalent of an annual income. Their defense against inflation is made simpler by the fact that all they need do is invest their money so that its yield equals or offsets the loss to inflation.

A person with $20,000 annual income who also has $20,000 in cash or liquid assets need only invest his $20,000 in assets at 5 per cent to produce enough money ($1,000 in this case) to overcome the erosion of inflation and the $1,000 increase in the cost of living.

Unfortunately, for most of us it's not as easy as that.

Yet, to face the problem squarely, the only way we can counteract inflation and protect ourselves against the rising cost of living is to invest assets.

To do this, we must acquire them.

Acquiring assets is not easy, particularly in a period of hurtful inflation, since for most of us, assets are accumulated through the tedious process of saving. Saving—it's almost a bad word these days.

To protect yourself against inflation, it's necessary to recognize—and accept—two facts. They are these:

1. The most direct way to combat inflation is through profitable investments that yield a return that is larger than the annual loss to inflation (larger than the rise in the cost of living).

2. The money you invest—unless you are uncommonly fortunate—must be salvaged from your annual earnings.

There emerges, then, a most distasteful fact. When what you earn in income buys less because of inflation, not only must you tighten your belt to accommodate *that* loss, you must tighten it even more in order to salvage more income so that it may be put to work partly to offset the "cost" of inflation.

"Salvage" is the word I prefer to "savings." Most of us have been imbued with the values of thrift, even though the figures show we don't practice what our teachers preached. "Savings" connotes an only slightly painful extraction of income to be squirreled away on a regular basis against a hatefully proverbial rainy day.

Savings are fine. They're necessary. They're hardly assets, because they're in escrow. They are escrowed against emergencies or contingencies at most, or escrowed against predictable expenses such as college educations or vacations, at the least.

They don't count. Forget them.

When you extract "asset" money from your income, it's bound to hurt.

It requires a tough discipline—tougher than you need to be a mere "saver."

Accept the fact that there's no way to "beat" inflation. You can checkmate it, if you make a supreme effort. You can counteract it to some degree under ordinary circumstances by exercising a reasonable amount of effort and doing a sensible amount of planning.

That's what this theme is all about. There is no valid reason for believing that things or conditions will change during the balance of the twentieth century. To the contrary, all signs point to a worsening of conditions. Therefore, it must be assumed that only individual effort will protect the average individual against the ravages of inflation. No government is coming to the rescue; no change of official attitudes or reversal of governmental policies can be expected to bring relief to the consumer in the area of constantly rising costs, especially of those things he must buy to survive or to make his survival comfortable.

After half a century dedicated to the ideological cause of providing security for the individual, the average urban American faces the bleak prospect of less security today than that afforded the sod–breaking pioneers who opened the West in territory that wasn't yet part of the United States.

The dirt farmers of the West of a century ago had some control over how much food and shelter they had.

The truth is, the modern urbanite has very little control over how much food and shelter he will have, for he has no control over how much his earned money will provide for him.

It is this that makes it necessary to "salvage." He must "salvage" all he can from his earned income, and put it to work against inflation.

That's because he is totally dependent on money—money, and nothing else—and money is rapidly losing its value.

Let's just examine how dependent you are on money, if you're an average American.

Every bit of food that your family consumes must be bought at a store or supermarket. Ah, perhaps you have a small garden—they used to call them "kitchen gardens"—but let's face it, its basic purpose is not to save your food costs but to provide you with fresher, better-tasting produce in season. Fact is, your home-grown food may cost you a bit more than you would pay in a supermarket.

You can't say—if you're average—that your home is your own. Either you rent it, as about half the families in America do, or you have a small equity in it. On a national average this runs to about 60 per cent equity owned by occupants, with the balance owned by mortgage lenders.

You can't make your own shoes, and, indeed, wouldn't know how to tan the hide if you had access to hides.

You can't weave the cloth for your clothes, and wouldn't know how to make thread if you owned wool-producing sheep and a busy colony of silkworms, along with a field of cotton.

The truth is, you can't even get very far from your present location, because you're so totally dependent on transportation.

Even the water you drink has to be paid for, either by yourself or by your landlord.

Never before in history has man been so abjectly dependent on money. Never before has his survival depended so totally on a continuing supply of money with a constant value.

If you are an average American you can provide nothing for yourself, not even drinking water, and you must rely on money to serve your every need.

You look at a dollar. You envision something. It is not a piece of paper, colored green. It is perhaps a pound of butter and a few cents in change, or one admission to a drive-in movie, or copies of *Esquire* and *Newsweek*.

It isn't what it was ten years ago when you looked at a dollar and saw two pounds of butter, admission to a drive-in for a whole family, and copies of *Time, Life, Esquire,* and *Newsweek*, with perhaps the *Saturday Evening Post*, too.

No, you say, a dollar isn't what it was.

Just remember that what it is today, it's not going to be tomorrow. It'll buy even less.

Translate it into everything you need in the way of food, clothing, shelter, transportation, medical care— every single thing that makes up life, living, sustenance, indeed, SURVIVAL—and you begin to have an idea of how important that money is to you.

So you must earn money, as much as you can.

Nothing new in that; everyone faces up to that task.

You must then protect yourself against inflation by taking two basic steps:

1. You must salvage money from your income.

2. You must use part of the salvaged income to play inflation's game—it must be put to work where it will *inflate itself* to offset in whole, or in part, what the current inflation is doing to your current earnings.

There is no other escape route.

The average American family saves less than 10 per cent of its income in two forms: life insurance and direct savings, forgetting, for the most part, that only a portion of the money paid in insurance premiums actually goes into a form of accruing savings.

Roughly speaking, though, the fellow with $100 per week income puts about $5 to $8 per week into an insurance program and the balance into savings, either a regular–dividend savings account or one of the modified versions. (There are many: day–of–deposit–day–of–withdrawal accounts; shares in a savings and loan association; modified certificates of deposit; etc.) The ratio of savings follows along general lines. The man who earns $200 a week puts about $10 per week into insurance and $10 into some kind of thrift program. A person with an income of $300 per week has insurance premiums of about $15 a week and a thrift program requiring $15 a week. And so on, until the upper brackets are reached where, believe it or not, the ratio falls off.

Those with the highest incomes save less proportionately than do those with the lower incomes. One reason for this is that they are obliged to spend more proportionately for one reason or another. They live in better homes, fancier neighborhoods, drive better cars, wear more expensive clothes, dine at better and costlier restaurants, send their children to more expensive schools, and even quite often seek out the most expensive physicians and dentists to care for their families' health.

This, they will argue, is for the sake of keeping up the necessary appearances for "The Job."

As a result, they have less money to put aside. This doesn't bother many of the high earners, however, for high income has a narcotic effect on the psyche. It is easy to believe that the income level will continue forever, so that when heads are lopped off in the great chess game of business and commerce, there is an instinctive protective emulsion that surges through the blood to coat the brain with the soothing message: "It can't happen to me."

Though they may not believe in poverty, the more successful denizens of the business world do believe in death. They buy huge insurance policies. They insure

themselves for prodigious amounts, making poten-
tially rich beneficiaries, in some cases, out of spouses
whom they detest and are planning to divorce.

By the time they're through making the necessary
payments to keep up appearances for "The Job," and
meeting the scheduled premium payments on their life
insurance programs, the well-to-do among us have very
little remaining for savings. Looking at the basic
figures from their lofty perches, many feel they would
be humiliated to put small weekly sums into a savings
account. It is beneath their income level, hence
beneath their dignity. Though many might well afford,
say, $25 a week in a savings account, they would feel
self-conscious about depositing such a paltry amount,
so they decide to save it themselves until they can
make a deposit of respectable size. They never do.
Something always happens to the money that is put
aside for this purpose. Experience shows that a self-
established escrow rarely works, even for the strong-
est-willed, best-disciplined executives.

What does rescue the well heeled from total degener-
ation of their earnings is the fact that they are also
substantial investors. Because of their income level,
their credit is good. This permits them to acquire equi-
ties in corporations on margin and through other credit
devices, and to acquire real estate holdings with substantial mortgages.

These two investments—common stocks of corporations and real estate—are the two best hedges against
inflation that are available to the average breadwinner.

Nevertheless, what the high-income earners have
been doing to protect themselves against inflation is, by
and large, not enough. They, too, must tighten their
belts. They, too, must embark on special inflation-
thwarting programs. When it comes to the basic use of
an income—for food, clothing, shelter and necessities—

all things are relative. A blue–collar worker who pays $80 a month for his mortgage is no less secure than the $1,000–a–week executive who pays $800 a month for his mortgage and $500 a month for the rent of his apartment in town (plus, probably, $300 a month for that delightfully secluded summer retreat).

All things are relative when it comes to the basics and the tycoon is just as reliant on money as is the hourly rated worker, and is just as vulnerable to its erosion. The tycoon, however, hires experts to advise him.

There is no escaping the fact, though, that inflation hits most cruelly at those of us in the lower brackets. We have less room to maneuver. If you erode 5 per cent from an income of $50,000, the high–bracket fellow can find ways to "adjust" for that loss of $2,500. But if you whack 5 per cent off an income of $5,000, the lost $250 is painfully missed.

The first inflation–fighting assignment for the man of modest or moderate means is to review his savings program. If he doesn't have one, shame on him; he'd better get started on one immediately, for it takes an entire year to get established in an inflation–controlling operation. A full year of saving has to pass before you can embark on any meaningful program. Your salvaged savings must have a full year of "seniority" on them before they start earning the rate of interest that is advertised for them.

When you see a thrift institution that advertises a 5 per cent dividend or interest on savings, you may think that here's an obvious way to stay even with the 5 per cent loss to inflation.

It would be, if you could draw all of your annual salary in advance, deposit it in such an institution, and find some other source of income for the full year. The full salary, nesting in that savings account, would produce five full percentage points of income, just about offsetting the loss of value of your money in recent years. You'd break even.

But let's face the facts. What are you "saving" now—about 10 per cent of your income, of which 5 per cent goes into direct savings? You are, if you're average.

If you earn $100 a week, you're keeping aside $10, of which $5 per week goes into your insurance programs and $5 goes directly into a savings account.

Savings institutions declare dividends on a quarterly basis, and their advertised annual rate is compounded quarterly. (Some call it the quarterly dividend; some term it quarterly interest; they're both the same.) These dividends are added in January for savings in the preceding October, November and December; in April, for savings in January, February and March; in July, for savings in April, May and June; and in October, for savings in July, August and September. There are thirteen weeks in each quarter.

If you started saving at the rate of $5 per week during the first week in January, you would have saved $65 by the end of March. Therefore in April, the bank would add 81 cents in interest, giving you a balance of $65.81. This is one–fourth of the 5 per cent annual rate, applied to your balance.

At the end of June you would have added another $65, and your balance would be $130.81. To this would be added the dividend of $1.64, boosting your balance to $132.45.

At the end of September you would have $197.45 in accumulated savings and interest, to which would be added the dividend of $2.47, bringing your balance to $199.92.

At year's end your total would stand at $264.92. In January the bank would add your dividend of $3.31, making your total for the year $268.23.

By peeling off $5.00 a week for savings, you have put aside a total of $260.00 out of your pay. You have earned dividends of $8.23.

This is nothing like 5 per cent. If you earned 5 per cent on $260, it would equal $13, and your total would stand at $273.

You can see that your money hasn't been "working" for you throughout the year, and therefore, only in its second year will it earn the full dividend.

In fact, when it comes to the harsh arithmetic, only the $5 that you deposited in the first week in January has been "working" for the full year. The bank has been most generous in counting the first $65 from the first quarter's deposits as being entitled to the full 5 per cent rate on a quarterly basis.

Yet, out of every $260.00 that you earned during the preceding year, you lost $13.00 to inflation and rising prices. You recovered part of it, $8.23, on one unit of $260.00

But $260 is only 1/20 of your annual pay of $5,200. You managed to recover a little more than half the inflationary loss on 1/20 of your income—but 19/20 of it, a total of $4,940, was subjected to the full impact.

If you compound that 5 per cent loss on a quarterly basis, which is about as fair a way as you can do it, this is what you find: From January through March you had earned $1,300.00, but your loss to inflation, calculated at one-quarter of 5 per cent, was $16.25, giving you net earnings, before taxes, of $1,283.75.

By June 30, you had added another $1,300.00 to your earnings, making the total $2,583.75. From this, inflation took another bite, knocking it down to $2,551.45.

In the third quarter your $1,300.00 earnings had brought the total up to $3,851.45, but inflation removed $48.16, bringing you back to $3,803.29.

At the end of the year you had added another $1,-

300.00 in earnings, bringing your total to $5,103.29. Inflation removed another $63.79, however, reducing your total to $5.039.50. That's what you earned in *real* money —before paying your taxes—for the entire year. It was $170.50 less than you had thought it would be.

You won't feel the full effect of the 5 per cent inflationary loss—$260.00—until the following year, when every penny you earn at $100 a week will be worth 5 per cent less than it was the year before. But by that time, the following year's inflationary erosion will be at work, too. If it, too, is at a rate of 5 per cent, your loss for that second year will be $430.50 (on the same basis), making your take–home pay—again, before paying your taxes—$4,769.50.

Let's take stock, now. You put aside some savings that in the first year earned you $8.23.

This is needed to help offset a minimum loss of $170.-50.

That's pretty ineffective offsetting, you must admit. You still have a net loss of $162.27.

Looking at it candidly, however, it isn't all that hard to make your money earn something like $162 in the course of a year.

Remember—the assignment isn't for you to *earn* an additional $162. That would be too easy, and it wouldn't be combating inflation. The trick is to have your *money* earn that $162. This brings us to the five cardinal rules for protecting yourself against inflation.

1. Cut down on your buying. Remember, your income is only partly *de*flated by inflation's impact. What is *in*flated is the cost of living. Prices are higher. What you don't buy won't hurt you.

2. Don't save your money for the purpose of buying some item. In periods of inflation, its cost will rise faster than your saved money will earn money.

3. Use your credit to its fullest to buy the items you

need and want (again, keeping them at a minimum). This way the burden of inflation is borne by the lender. He gets repaid in cheapening dollars, customarily at a fixed rate of interest.

4. Save more out of your income than you have ever done before, despite high prices, and put it where you will get a maximum rate of return.

5. Invest more out of your savings than you ever have, looking for inflation–proof investments of the kind that will be explored in this book.

The one sure way to beat inflation is not to buy anything at inflated prices.

Since you can't avoid doing that for many goods and services, you are left with one alternative: cut down on what you do buy.

The first and most important item in inflation–jousting is paying for your shelter. If you are renting, your living costs are mounting rapidly unless you're one in a million. Rents generally, even those under some form of control, have been climbing steadily for the last quarter of a century. Even the enormous increases posted on many rental properties are not enough, the landlords say, to compensate for the boosts in real estate taxes and maintenance costs, including the increasing cost of mortgage money (which most landlords have to contend with). No matter how high you think your rent is now, chances seem good that you'll be paying higher rental in the future.

If you're renting, then, the first investment you should consider is a home of your own, be it a private house in suburbia, a duplex or garden apartment in the metropolitan area, or a cooperative or a condominium in the city. Then part of what you're paying in rent each month will be paid to yourself. It's not a form of forced saving, as many contend, but rather a form of forced investment. Your house is of value as a home, of course, but its only monetary value comes when it is sold and you convert your forced investment to cash.

Just remember, you can't live in a building constructed of dollar bills.

You'll have to buy or otherwise provide for some new shelter when you sell your house.

Viewing your investment in your home realistically, it's more an investment for your estate than it is for your own portfolio. A home is of value only when it is resold, and you can't afford to sell it if after doing so you have to buy another home at inflated prices.

The trick here, of course, is to hold onto your home as long as you possibly can without moving to newer or better or larger or more expensive quarters.

If you've had a mortgage for several years, you're paying a much lower rate of interest than those who are buying homes today.

Mortgage money can't be expected to get cheaper in the foreseeable future, so, by all means, hold onto your present home as long as you can. If you don't have one, get one as soon as you can.

There may come a time when you're ready for retirement or after your family has grown and left home that you can sell your present home and move into a smaller, less expensive one, thus providing yourself with some handsome cash assets in the transaction. That's something to count on in long–range planning and it is part—a small part—of the assault on inflation over the long haul. Small though its role may be, it's an important step, perhaps the most important.

There are many goods and services you must buy, even at inflated prices. Basic foods and basic clothes, of course, are on that list, but most people spend foolishly in both categories. Medical bills, dental bills, tuition costs, transportation costs are among those expenses that are difficult to control.

But your basic challenge is unalterable. You must save more money so that you can invest more money. In order to save more, you must buy less; you must use less of your income for those rising costs of living.

A good place to start is with food. The cost of food, incidentally, customarily leads all other categories in posting annual inflationary price increases.

Most people have fallen into expensive habits when purchasing family groceries. The processors and packagers have made it all so easy, so convenient, so attractive, that the displays in the supermarkets almost beckon to you as you pass by with your grocery cart. It's all very effective and it has made many millionaires in the food processing, distributing and retailing industries.

It is time here to face an unpleasant truth about the modern housewife. She has quit her job as helpmeet, or at best is giving the job only passing attention.

In the old days when dad was out hustling a dollar, he knew that his mate was back home doing everything in her power to preserve that dollar intact; doing all she could to keep household expenses—particularly food costs—at a minimum.

The wife of today finds that everything is done for her. Her foods are prepackaged, all ready to heat and serve. Some need only to be unwrapped. Maybe you husbands haven't been paying attention but it has been carried to the point where even breakfast cereal is presugared to save milady the task of sprinkling a spoonful of sugar on Junior's corn flakes. This sugared cereal costs more than the unsugared kind. Every "prepared" item that comes from the grocery costs more than would be the case if the housewife did more of the work herself and left less to the processors and packagers.

While they're preparing mom's food for her to heat and serve to dad and the family, she is devoting more time to being a family chauffeur and a local committeewoman, chores that drain off additional dollars from the family budget.

There will be many wives who will accuse me of being an old grouch, but I think most of them will be fair–minded enough to admit that the weekly food bill could be cut considerably with a little more work in the kitchen before the meals are served.

I'll go so far as to suggest that a good housewife will be able to think of many more cost-cutting items than I—a mere man—am able to list herein.

If you want to cut down on your food bills so that you can save more to fight inflation, here are a few things to avoid buying:

· Canned spaghetti. Make your own; it'll taste better and serve many more.

· Canned baked beans. They're a poor imitation of the very inexpensive potful you can make with just a little practice.

· Fresh fruits. The canned and frozen varieties are just about as good and much less expensive in most cases.

· Fresh vegetables. Frozen and canned vegetables are fully as good as the aged, overgrown varieties found at most produce counters, and they are generally less expensive.

· Ready–made cakes, cookies and candy. Make your own.

· Cake mixes. Your own mix costs just about half.

· Fancied–up cereals. Get the old-fashioned dry kind. Avoid sugar–treated cereals.

· Desserts. There are no cheap ones around anymore. Make your own. Suggestions follow.

· Bread. No bread is a good buy. It is no longer the item it once was. Today's supermarket bread, sold at an outrageous price, couldn't be the staff of life for a grasshopper. Make your own, or do without. If you are willing to bake your own, try making a double or triple batch and freezing it.

· Prepared specialty items. Take pizzas, for instance. If your family wants pizza you can make your own at probably one–quarter of the cost of the average prepared item.

· Fish. Beware, for you probably think this continues to be one of the most inexpensive food items. Not any more. We are giving, at no cost whatsoever, our school fish to the Russian fishing fleet, and as a result almost all fish is as expensive as meat. The one exception is canned tuna, but Latin American countries are harassing American tuna fleets with the result that tuna, too, will soon increase in cost.

Meat is the mainstay of any diet, and it can't be avoided at the supermarket, but it can be purchased on a much sounder basis than is customarily the case. Most meats still have seasonal fluctuations in prices, and the wise housewife will note the bargains in the newspaper ads and plan her menus accordingly.

Fat fowls are usually among the less expensive meat items. Careful planning can parlay a good fat chicken into several wholesome, tasty, family–pleasing meals. Strangely, bologna is a good buy much of the time, though its little relative, the hot dog, has been priced into the luxury class. Many hot dogs continue to have questionable composition. They may taste fine, but, with some, you might not like them so much if you knew what was stuffed into that skin.

It takes planning first, and some hard kitchen work afterwards, but more careful shopping can put many extra dollars into the savings account each week.

The first step is the preparation of a shopping list. A woman without one is like a pilot without a compass. She is distracted by everything that catches her eye— or her fancy. She becomes an impulse–buyer, the delight of every store manager. The more impulse–buyers he has in his community, the sooner he'll be able to retire and take it easy.

The second step is to get to know prices. A woman should enter a supermarket knowing about how much she intends to spend.

I strongly recommend that she take along one of those little hand tabulators to keep score. They cost only a dollar or two and can save that amount week after week.

There's another reason you need the little tallying gadget. It's plainly silly to believe that every checkout cashier is impervious to making mistakes, or that every single one is completely honest. If your mission is scouting out every dollar you can lay hands on, the checkout counter is a good place to start.

When it comes to planning meals, the housewife should give consideration to some good, nourishing stews that are inexpensive and easy to make. They'll also fill the house with a savory pungency that will draw the family to the table with no urging.

Chicken dishes, egg dishes, rice dishes are also economical and easy to prepare and have the virtue of being adaptable to numerous tasty varieties.

Dealing with leftovers can also be a source of satisfaction to the housewife who is eager to help. Some enticing casseroles can be concocted, or, for the timid, there are legions of recipes in the better cookbooks.

There are no inexpensive desserts to be found in today's stores. You'd do well to make your own. Cakes or pies that are "made from scratch" by the housewife are not expensive. Good puddings can be made at low cost. Jello remains a bargain, and some grades of ice cream are low in price, calories and quality, though they taste fine.

Since these instructions really deal with "How To Be A Well–Organized Cheapskate," why not let that policy be your guide when it comes to selecting fresh fruits and vegetables? Go to the source. Go out into the country, in season, and get 'em where they grow.

In the first place, supermarkets allow for a certain percentage of spoilage. They hope they'll sell all of their fresh produce, but they have adjusted prices and inventories and shipments so that a certain quantity can be thrown away without severe monetary loss.

The local farmers aren't geared that way. They have to sell what they grow or turn it into fodder or compost. When it is ready for market, it's there. Nothing can be done about holding it back or slowing down the amount.

This is where the good shopper gets her bargains. Not only is the quality far superior, but prices are lower and with a little bit of semihaggling, both price and quantity can be flexible in a way that redounds to the buyer's favor.

There are also such things as "seconds" that are perfectly all right. These are slightly blemished specimens. They don't command top price, yet they taste just as good and will store just as well as the more expensive kinds. This applies to the sturdier fruit-vegetable varieties such as apples, pears, peaches, citrus fruits, cherries, tomatoes, cabbages, squash, cucumbers, melons, and some other fresh vegetables.

Out in the countryside there's also a new development in merchandising that saves a considerable amount of money. The customer picks his own produce at the farmer's lot, and since labor costs are saved, pays a much lower price. He can do this with strawberries, blueberries, raspberries, blackberries, cherries, grapes, and even sweet corn. In this way there's no sacrifice as to grade or quality, and it provides a family treat, along with a family outing, at a greatly reduced cost.

The foregoing muses on but a few ways that a wife, intent on helping her husband save those hard–earned dollars, can contribute mightily to the savings account, that necessary foundation from which inflation–proof security is built.

There must be hundreds of other ways that a wife can cut costs by planning her menus, planning her shopping forays, and then buying with a hard, eagle's eye to price.

Nobody promises that it will be fun.

But the rewards will be worth it.

The real problem of dealing with inflation is that you have money to spend and it's likely to weigh heavily in your pocket—or, as the old-timers used to say, "burn holes in your pocket"—trying to get spent.

When the nation's economy is in trouble because of a depression, most people are short on money. That's when they economize. It's a time when, for the sake of correcting the economy's ills, they should buy more and spend more. When inflation troubles the economy, they should buy less and spend less. Yet with money in their pockets, at the time of inflation, people are prone to spend more.

What you have to do, then, is cultivate the habit of contrary thinking. Swim upstream, away from the crowd. Be an opposite. When everybody is economizing it is time for you to spend. That's when you'll get your best buys—in everything from shelter to clothes to cars to education. When everyone is spending and generally living it up, that is the time for you to cut back, squirrel it away, sock it in the bank, and prudently invest. Pile up your assets for the day when the world is filled with bargains. If you do all your buying during a period of inflation, you are merely proving that P.T. Barnum was right in his assessment of the human race when he observed that "a sucker is born every minute." And don't forget what W. C. Fields had to say about that: "Never give a sucker an even break."

Assignment: Spend less.

Question: How?

In addition to food the areas for potential belt-tightening are scarce. The three biggest items remaining are:

Clothing

Transportation

Entertainment

Take clothing, for instance. Offered to suffering mankind on a silver platter was a great opportunity to improvise in clothing, an opportunity presented by the hippies, yippies and other assorted dissenters who most properly protested the modern code that required blind adherence and subservience to current style, an ever-changing chameleon. For the first time since the Indian tribes roamed the American glades, they, the pacesetters, welcomed improvisations in style.

They almost—but not quite—made it possible for:

· A fellow in a sleeveless shirt to borrow money from a bank.

· A lawyer to go to work without wearing a hat.

· A commuter to ride a train in a white shirt without a tie.

· An honest, hard–working person to walk down Fifth Avenue on a summer's hottest day without wearing a tie and jacket and still not be branded a tourist.

· A steady patron to eat in a white–tablecloth restaurant without having to wear a tie in New York, Boston, Philadelphia, Washington, Miami, Chicago, Milwaukee, Minneapolis, St. Louis, Kansas City, New Orleans, Houston, Dallas, Phoenix, Denver, Omaha, Portland, Seattle, San Francisco, Oakland, Sacramento, Los Angeles and San Diego.

· An adult to wear sneakers on a subway or bus.

· A theatre patron to wear Hush–Puppies, those inexpensive, comfortable shoes that so shatteringly frighten the snobs.

· A beach–goer to wear old clothes to get all sandy and salty, rather than special resort clothes.

All of this might have happened, thanks to the protesters, except for two things:

1. They rapidly became conformists, and when one prominent yippie wore an old Nazi field jacket, it became *de rigueur* for every well–dressed yippie to affect an old Nazi field jacket. This sent Seventh Avenue to its cutting tables and sewing machines making, of all improbable things, Nazi field jackets, which were dispatched in all haste to the "underground retailers" so that yippies from coast to coast and border to border could conform.

2. At the same time, the over–thirty generation reacted bitterly, failing totally to realize that it had been liberated from idiotic style compulsions, and the nonyippies insisted that all white–tablecloth diners wear shirts and ties, that no turtlenecks be worn at Toots Shor's, the Twenty–One or the Harvard Club, (thus making them outlawed throughout the entire world of white tablecloths), that sneaker–wearers be banned forthwith, and that Hush–Puppie citizens be seated in a segregated place.

Heaven forbid that we should spend less for our clothes, or that the male species should be comfortable when he "dresses up."

We killed our style revolution before it really got started.

It cost us all a great deal of money. Now we have to wage a revolution on an individual basis.

Here's something for you men to think about the next time the thermometer gets over 90 degrees. If you're wearing a shirt and tie, you have fashioned exactly thirteen thicknesses of cloth around your neck. At the collar seam the cloth is double–folded and stitched together, making four thicknesses. To this is added the double thickness of the cloth of the collar. The total now is six thicknesses. The collar is turned over, doubling its thickness—add two more thicknesses for a total of eight. Now between the two folds of the collar you have a tie. It is of double thickness to begin with, and is folded over and stitched, making four additional thicknesses, for a total of twelve thicknesses around your neck. In most ties there is a linen binder inside— add at least one more thickness of cloth, for a grand total of thirteen.

Fashion decrees that if you are indoors you may loosen both tie and collar, but if you're going outside into the hot sunlight, you must pull all thirteen thicknesses of cloth tight around your neck.

If anyone can make any sense out of this "style," I'd be grateful for any enlightenment.

As you stroll out into the hot sun, you slip into your suit coat that, if it is of standard construction, has a doubled-over collar with felt or flannel lining underneath, adding four more thicknesses of heavy cloth to your suffering neck.

For your tie you paid anywhere from $1 to $25. Your dress shirt cost anywhere from $4 to $25. You have robbed from your salvageable money anywhere from $5 to $50 so that you may have the privilege of running the risk of heat prostration.

A less inhibited fellow or one whose job doesn't require such formality can walk down that same sunny street wearing a sleeveless, open–neck attractive slip–on jersey that he purchased for less than $2.

We've been deluded into thinking that the chap with the shirt, tie and jacket is the one who is getting ahead in this world, while the poor slob in the comfortable jersey isn't.

Maybe that's the way it is, too—but the fellow in the short-sleeved, open–neck sportshirt has a far better chance to sock some of his clothing allowance into savings than does the perspiring aspirer who harnesses his neck with thirteen thicknesses of cloth in order to walk down to the shoeshine parlor on the corner.

Obviously what is needed is another style revolution, one conducted by genuine revolutionaries who won't subsequently conform and who won't panic when fingers of scorn are pointed in their direction.

One looks to the youth to lead such revolutions, but experience has shown that youth chickens out somewhere along the way. Remember the zoot suit? Remember the failure of the men's shorts–at–business experiment?

Someone who leads a style revolution with economy as the goal may not win a plaque from the London Tailor's Guild, but he should get a special citation from the Secretary of the Treasury as the person who contributed substantially to the control of inflation.

Much as a revolt is needed in men's wear, the requirement is twice as great when it comes to women's styles.

Anyone who observes the economics of female fashions, rather than the details of the style change, will realize that it follows a dollar–draining pattern, based on a scheme that makes milady's wardrobe obsolete as soon as it is fully stocked. There are built–in tricks, too, that are employed periodically to forestall any effort to make clothes modish by remodeling or alterations.

Just prior to World War II the garment manufacturers enjoyed a little style jockeying by playing with hemlines. They were long one year and short the next. The manufacturers found that this gave them a two–year spread before wardrobes became obsolescent. If the hemline was lowered in one year, the owners of the longer dresses could themselves shorten them the following year, if style decreed that the hemline move upward a couple of inches. The next year when they were lowered again, however, milady had to rush out to restock her wardrobe. She could shorten dresses with scissors, needle and thread, but she couldn't very well lengthen them once they had been abbreviated.

When war broke out the government decreed that the skirts of ladies in uniform should be one inch below the knee, hoping that it was a hemline that would become countrywide, if not universal. The industry, busy with war orders, conformed. Hardly had V–J Day been observed, however, when the new postwar styles were announced. Skirts were to be longer. Midcalf, for a start. You couldn't adapt any of those wartime models to that style. Whole new wardrobes had to be purchased. A year later the hemline dropped two inches lower to a "fashionable" two to four inches above the ankles!

Those with long memories may recall that when skirts were shortened again, a couple of years later, bodices and necklines also changed. This was to prevent any attempt merely to cut off some cloth and shorten the garments.

Through the years it can be noted that whenever women's fashions are shortened, the neckline, bodice or silhouette is changed—sometimes all three. This inhibits the girls who think they can fight Seventh Avenue or the Paris salons with their Singers or Necchis. It might be done, but it's not easy.

Faced with the situation, how, then, does an average housewife—or an average breadwinner—practice thrift and fight inflation while remaining suitably clothed?

I asked a lady who, in my opinion, is one of the nation's leading experts at the art of stretching the clothing dollar. Buoyant and in middle age, she has five children, runs a large home quite efficiently and is married to a man whose income has abrupt peaks and valleys because of his occupation, which is writing.

She's my wife, Marge, and she has tendered the following memo in response to my query:

"Dear D. I.:

I think the most important first step for a thrift-minded housewife to take is to get a good, reliable mail order catalog, such as Sears, Roebuck; Montgomery Ward; Spiegel's; or Cooley's. Find the mail-order house that you trust as offering a moderate price range for serviceable or durable goods. It can become a sort of blue book in giving you a point of reference, a place to do your own comparison shopping.

When some item of clothing is needed, I look it up in our catalog and get an idea as to price, then I check the local department stores and specialty shops. Sometimes I uncover excellent bargains locally. Other times I find that the catalog item is the best buy, so I send in a telephone order. This way I'm bound to save some money, and I rarely have to indulge in what I call 'shopping blind'.

Stay away from extremes in style unless you want to splurge. If you're intent on saving money—as you must be if you want to fight the effects of inflation—think like, plan like and shop like Sensible Sal. Our policy is to have a good but *basic* wardrobe. We add new items only when wear or some special occasion makes it necessary.

We like to buy the best quality for those items that we use most, such as everyday shoes, business suits for father (and his shirts and ties, too) and the basics for mom and the kids.

The best quality has to be bought in such items as an 'everywhere suit' for mother, well designed and adaptable, and a 'crisis dress' that can be used on almost any occasion, expected or otherwise.

Overcoats and winter coats for both father and mother should be of excellent quality and style because they will be worn for several years. (Remembering this will help you keep your weight in line.) There are other highest-quality items you will buy on a thrift program, but more about that later.

When it comes to shopping for children, it's a different matter.

Let's start right at the top and consider teenagers. They will not economize, no matter what inducements you offer. Teenagers invented faddism and are its most devout practitioners. Unchecked, they will support nearly every new fad in styles that comes along; they'd never buy the basics by themselves, and soon they'd have you running to the loan sharks to borrow money to buy platinum–and–chartreuse sandals that simply *must* be acquired before Debbie has her party.

We have found there is only one realistic way to deal with teenagers. We buy the basic blue suit and basic accessories for our boy, and basic 'dressed–up' dress and accessories for our girl. These are held to be almost sacred garments, to be worn only on command from mother or for some ultraspecial occasion.

Then we give each an allowance. It is adequate to buy their school and everyday clothing, and to provide some entertainment such as movies and some snacks such as bubble gum or, as I discovered with Dave, an entire pizza, designed for a family of four.

They can splurge it all on cokes and offbeat clothes if they wish. The time comes soon, however, when they learn, sorrowfully and with much loud lament, that it's unwise to indulge in every fad that comes along.

This works only if you resolve in the beginning to be tough about it when Nancy comes to you and asks for a supplemental allowance to buy sneakers so she can go on an overnight hike and camping trip with the girls in her class, confessing that all she has are purple pool shoes and some sandals that match only her new sunburst–and–gold slacks.

Let her walk the two miles to the campsite in her sandals just once and she'll acquire an immediate appreciation for serviceability in footgear and place smaller value on the frilly stuff. Not that she shouldn't have the sandals if she wants them; but only if first she has provided for sneakers. She has to learn to plan ahead. That's the whole trick of inflation–fighting— planning ahead—and the sooner your offspring learn to take on the assignment, the better off they'll be. And you, too.

When I say we provide the basics, I mean just that. We do buy the required shoes for our teenagers. These are of the finest quality. They are for school, for church, for 'going out' with mom and dad.

The special 'dress-up' shoes for Nancy that match her best party dress are the lowest price–and–quality shoes we can find. We figure that they'll be worn only a few hours, and if not discarded with an 'ugh!' will soon be outgrown, anyway.

We buy the fundamentals such as underwear, socks and such at a place where we have come to trust the quality, reliability and wearability, and know that the price is, at most, moderate. Nobody checks the brand name of kids' underwear or socks.

This is true of adults, too. When you see pictures of important people being greeted by the President in the Oval Room of the White House, you may note that they are tastefully attired, but you never know whether their undergarments bear labels saying Sears, Grant's,

Woolworth's or Penney's—and you don't care, now, do you?

Before we abandon the subject of sneakers, let's make a mental note about them: Buy the cheapest kind you can find. Not so long ago it was worthwhile to buy some of the name brands of highest reputation. They were made of good–quality, long–lasting material, and would stand by a youngster throughout the summer months and on into gym classes at school in the fall until, ultimately, they were outgrown. Today, however, no sneakers last very long, irrespective of the price you pay, so you might as well get the least costly.

There was a time when we thought it necessary to have at least a two-week supply of such necessities as socks, underwear and handkerchiefs, because half of them would be in the laundry for a week. With today's washers and dryers, however, such a large supply is not needed. A three- or four-day supply of these essentials will see you through to the next washing.

It should be noted parenthetically that for the average family, an automatic washer and dryer are necessary investments for the inflation–battling campaign. Laundries have priced themselves into the luxury class, and their service is so slow that it cannot compete with automated equipment in the home.

Expensive as laundries have become, dry cleaners have grown even worse. Only the very rich should patronize them regularly.

We try to avoid garments that won't wash easily. We even duck those that need ironing. One of the marvels of modern science, is the 'wash and wear' sizing that is put into fibers, and it's a wasteful housewife who doesn't take maximum advantage of this economic and convenient item.

While I'm confessing that I don't iron much, let me also admit that I don't like to sew and do as little of it as possible. Not that I'm any lily of the field, but I've found that by the time I'm through constructing something on my sewing machine, I have invested as much in money and time as it would cost to buy the professionally sewn article in the store, thanks to the mass–production principle. You can buy a car for a relatively low price because manufacturers produce thousands of the same model. To construct one by yourself would cost many times the price you pay. The same holds true with clothes, unless, of course, you are especially gifted as a seamstress, and can turn out something to shame Ceil Chapman and Sophie Gimbel.

Clothes should be bought more to fit your way of life than to fit your aspirations and dreams. Think about that. How often do you appear in public? Are you the star of the show? Or are you part of the background?

We have both types in our family. Father is often required to be the speaker at large gatherings, sometimes formal affairs, and quite often he makes guest appearances on television shows. He probably averages three important business luncheons a week where he has to look his best, either because he's lunching in what he calls an 'expense account restaurant,' or because he has to impress whomever he's dining with.

We rarely economize on his 'working gear.' His overcoat is fine dark blue cashmere (it's light, won't wrinkle, won't show spots, and is always in style). His suits are made by a good tailor, as are his shirts—a dozen at a time (shirts, not suits, that is).

He buys his ties at Sulka's, his hats at Cavanaugh's, and his shoes at Whitehouse & Hardy, where they keep a cast of his feet.

This isn't an expenditure. It's an investment, for his appearance could quite likely determine how well we live, and govern our way of life.

Underneath all of that expensive attire, however, are

undergarments and socks that come from *my* favorite
mail-order house, a firm that has provided us with quality, long–wearing merchandise at modest prices for
many years. Our family, in fact, has mail–shopped
there for generations, usually with satisfying results.
All right, I'll break down and reveal that it's Sears,
though I suspect that Monkey Ward and others, such as
Spiegel's, are just as good. The only way a mail-order
house can stay in business these days, when shopping
centers dot even the most remote sections of our land,
is to offer very good quality at a reasonable price.

Father's gardening outfits come from Sears, too. And
he's a genuine gardener, an organic buff, who wallows
in mud and dust from the last frost to the first snow.

He has two grades of sports outfits. One, moderate–
priced, casual, comfortable, is for wear around our ul-
tracasual, ultracomfortable suburban home. The other
is more formal resort wear, for use in wintertime in
Florida, the islands, Arizona or some such spot where
the escapees from the north winds might wish him to
make a speech or put in some kind of appearance.

The resort clothes, however, are bought in New York
at the end of the summer season, when they're marked
down. Their prices are much, much higher when
bought at the winter resorts.

Now we come to mom, a nongadabout, a nonclub-
woman, a non–do–gooder, but a typical housewife and
mother, a close and loving mate of a fairly successful
and extremely busy husband, and the 'treasurer' of the
outfit, charged with managing the money the breadwinner brings in. (This *is* the ideal arrangement, isn't
it?)

I think I'm quite typical. There are literally millions
of women situated just as I am. It makes little difference what the husband does for a living, the effects on
the wife and family are just the same. If a husband

sells mutual funds or cars or insurance or real estate; if he is a public relations man, an advertising man, a doctor, a dentist, a druggist or a florist, the management of the family budget, insofar as the wife is concerned, comes out just about the same. An IBM wife faces the same problems that I do. So does a pilot's wife. So does the wife of a man who drives a truck, or operates a crane or a bulldozer.

I need a good, high–quality Fifth Avenue dress, and one good, wrinkle–proof, expensive–looking dark suit. These are my 'crisis clothes.' They are most suitable for being the 'speakers' wife,' which often requires standing in a receiving line or sitting at a head table, or for impressing a publisher's representative who may be interested in a new story outline, or for that grand evening out when the delayed check finally arrives and a splurge and night at the theatre seem in order. The suit is useful for weddings, funerals, christenings, bar mitzvahs or an unscheduled trip for some unexpected reason.

These garments are my expensive ones. They are bought at my favorite specialty shops where, to be truthful, most customers never look at the price.

I look at the prices, because I'm trained to fight inflation. When I do, I shudder. But then I remind myself that these are special clothes. They are necessary. As far as the dress is concerned, it's almost in the category of a working garment. My husband wouldn't go far if, when addressing the Ladies' Auxiliary of the Dandelion Lovers of America, he had to introduce as his wife a frowsy female fresh off the cabbage patch in Connecticut. I can't overwhelm the good ladies of Flagstopp, but believe me, they're just as critical and discerning as the most jet–sated Park Avenue hostess. I have to look pretty damned kempt. And couth.

And when it comes to the suit, I remind myself that

we wouldn't want to bury dear old Aunt Mehitable with me appearing in a Hooverette or my favorite gardening–housecleaning–garage-straightening–up dress. Nor can you show up at such an occasion in a slinky number calculated to make the male mourners forget their loss.

These are crisis clothes. They cost money.

Underneath them are serviceable things from Sears.

Beneath them are shoes so cheap your instinct is to pass them by and leave them for the unfortunates.

My high–quality shoes are for everyday, constant wearing. I don't want foot problems. They're extremely expensive, and they're extremely comfortable.

The shoes I buy to match my head-table gown *look* expensive, but they're junk. Why not? Nobody is going to get down on all fours to inspect them. And the truth is, I'll wear them only on special occasions for a few hours at a stretch, and back they will go in the shoe rack in my closet.

When it comes to really dressing up, the inexpensive shoes alone are inflation–busters. I go all-out on accessories. I spend top money for handbags, gloves, hats, earrings and jewelry. Other women notice these things. Men don't; but women dress for women. They do it so their husbands can feel proud, or at least comfortable, among other wives. It's vicious, but there it is. Nothing will change it, not even galloping inflation.

I have to admit there's a bit of satisfaction in seeing the look in the eye of my husband when he sees me all dressed up in my best. Lots of times he acts a little surprised.

Most of the time he sees me around the place in everyday clothes that come from local shops and chain stores. They have to be wash and wear (no dry cleaning, no ironing) and, of course, I try to get them as becoming as possible; but to be frank, I don't think I'd ever be photographed as Housewife of the Month by *Women's Day* or *Family Circle* magazines. And t'hell with snobs, for underneath it's all Sears, Grant's and Penney's.

There are other areas where I splurge and buy the very best. My winter coat is chosen with the utmost care, and price has no bearing. It is intended to last several seasons. I avoid extremes of any kind, and, perhaps because of taste, tend toward the neutral or quiet colors. Warmth and practicability are major considerations, for after all, we live in New England where the winters are real. Our home may be within commuting distance of Times Square, but the elevation and latitude remind us annually for at least two months, sometimes three, that the Middle Atlantic States end at Port Chester.

I also buy a raincoat of excellent quality and style. Such a garment, of superior grade, lasts several years. It's a necessity in an area such as ours where there is much rain, for it is a pity to get all dressed up to meet someone of importance to my husband's career and then find I have to cover it all up with shabby–looking raingear.

We do a great deal of our major shopping in late summer. My husband likes to wear light–weight suits throughout the year, even when the outside thermometer is well below freezing, so we like to browse through the late-season bargains in summer suits and resort wear. If we're lucky we get to Florida in the winter. Our resort wear has all been purchased in late summer at marked–down prices in Manhattan or Connecticut.

It's unnecessary to point out, I suspect, that a wife who is also a breadwinner can't possibly indulge in the same buying techniques that I use. However, she can pattern her wardrobe-building after my husband's. When it's necessary to dress well, it's not necessary to shop wastefully.

Of all items of apparel, I think shoes are the most important, not merely for appearance, but for comfort and wearability. Throughout our family, the most expensive shoes are the ones we wear the most. Our dress shoes are inexpensive and can be replaced as fashions change without causing problems to our budget.

When my husband is working at the typewriter, he wears his beloved Hush–Puppies, and claims that his 'feet are wreathed in smiles.' When he's working, say, giving a speech, he wears his expensive custom–made shoes. Try standing at a podium in one spot for ninety minutes sometime, and you'll see why.

In the foregoing you have detected, I'm sure, the basic governing principle for the prudent outfitting of a family. With the certain exceptions that are noted, it boils down to this:

Buy the highest quality when you:

· Must appear at your best in public.

· Want the utmost in comfort and serviceability (that is, shoes).

Buy medium quality, at moderate prices when you:

· Don't care whose name appears on the label.

· Seek quality and quantity for a price, as in buying everyday socks for all the men in the family.

· Expect to subject the apparel to pretty tough treatment, such as housework or gardening or, in the case of children, playing.

Buy lowest quality, at lowest prices when you:

· Try to keep up with a fad or extreme style change.

· Buy exact–match accessories to go with one garment.

· Buy evening shoes or special–occasion footwear.

· Need some frilly morale booster, to break the monotony of continuously prudent shopping. Don't *always* be practical, but don't let yourself get carried away.

Now these are operating rules for adults. For children, it's quite something else again. The subject is so exhaustive I've asked my husband for an additional chapter to deal with it. Coming up, then: the most prudent way to outfit kids."

10. Before They Are Teenagers

Many of us grew up in an era when our winter coats had to bear Fifth Avenue labels, or the hallmark of the most exclusive store in the city nearest to us. If this brand of distinction wasn't apparent, you were just out of it. If they're given sufficient coaching by their parents, children can be absolute and horrible snobs, even little ones.

Just as they have to be taught to hate, they also have to be taught to be snobs.

Left to their own judgment, kids care little about labels, don't recognize the difference between a dime and a ten–dollar bill, and fail to realize that there's much difference between Woolworth's and Bergdorf's.

I'll tell you something. If you spot a kid with snobbish clothes, he has a snob for a mother. Quite likely she's *nouveau*, y'know, and is trying to impress.

What small children want in clothes is something that fits comfortably. They also have their own preferences in colors, a fact that is ignored by too many mothers.

If a mother meets those two standards—comfort and color—she can be as practical as she wishes in dressing a small child up to five years of age, possibly even seven.

This is where it pays to be practical, particularly if there are younger children growing up close behind.

There are certain items of children's apparel that can be bought with the full intention of having them passed along to younger members of the family when the original owner outgrows them.

These include:
· Winter coats
· Rain slickers
· Sweaters
· Sports jackets or snow jackets
· Some party dresses
· Some dress–up boy's suits
· Surviving boots

Articles that are purchased with the intention of having them passed along when the original wearer outgrows them must be chosen carefully, as to quality and style or color. Avoid extreme styles. Stick with moderate, acceptable colors. It can be crushing if a small friend chirps up with: 'O–ho, that purple coat used to be your sister's.' Said friend may never notice or comment if it's a good, neutral grey.

Such a garment should be washable. Yes, even the winter coats are capable of going in with the family wash these days. First you must read the label carefully, however.

Care should be taken to see that it's not a bulky garment. Children hate to be buttoned into an outfit that leaves them barely able to move, yet you see so many of them struggling off to the school bus looking like little space men, their arms outthrust uncomfortably, their legs waddling along in unyielding folds of cloth.

If a coat, a slicker, a sweater can be passed along to the next child, you should pay less attention to price and more to quality and the durability factor. There is no need, though, to strive for elegance, merely because you're unfettered by price restrictions.

When buying socks or mittens I recommend buying two pairs of each for each child, preferably all the same color and style. Then when one is lost, there's no great tragedy. Even a second and third can disappear—and they will—but you won't be out of socks or mittens that match. In these days of stretch yarns, universal sizes fit all small hands and feet comfortably. It's wasteful not to take full advantage of these marvels of modern science, which are, by the way, totally washable.

When buying knit shirts, get the best quality. They are worn all year long and can be subjected to innumerable washings.

Sometimes tights are needed for the severe winter weather. When buying these, get the cheapest. They don't wash too well, and when there's the inevitable fall and tear in the knee, they are through. We tried sewing a torn knee, but it was an astonishingly unsuccessful venture.

Ideally, each child should have five school (or play) outfits. These include four tops and four skirts that can be interchanged, for our girl, and four shirts or jerseys, or both, to go with three or four pairs of slacks, for our boy. Then there's a jumper for the girl, for that day when she's in the school play or goes on what the teacher calls a 'field trip' to the museum.

The girl must have an excellent party dress and the boy needs a fine–quality dress suit. These come from the top-quality store. The party dress that can be bought in a local chain may be in fashion today, but won't remain in style for even the three or four wearings in store for it. So when it comes to 'dress-ups,' buy the best, and just hope that they can be passed down the line to the family members who are growing up.

We find that the much–vaunted and hallowed tradition of buying a new Easter coat is a genuine luxury and should not be included in the budget of a woman intent on inflation–fighting. The young man or young girl who gets an Easter coat wears such finery only three or four times, at most, before it's outgrown. In many latitudes a coat may be necessary at Easter but summer is not far off when coats go into moth-balls.

I do agree, however, that some sort of outer coat is needed. Little Sally can look mighty peculiar going to a party all gussied up in her fanciest dress but wearing her sister's ski jacket.

Try looking for that combination raincoat–topcoat that now comes in high fashion styles and in good, usable colors. They can be worn all year and can double for covering party dresses, going to church or to other special occasions.

It's good to have an inflexible rule about school clothes. No matter how worn they may be or how near the finish line they are considered, insist that they be changed for play clothes just as soon as your child returns home from school.

We buy children's underwear, sleepwear, socks and hankies at our local store if prices compare favorably with those in the mail-order catalogs. If not, we send away for them. Socks are about the cheapest we can buy. They get lost, chewed by the dog or scuffed full of holes so soon after purchase that it's a waste of money to buy good quality. Robes are quickly outgrown and rarely passed along. We get terry cloth robes, medium quality, because they can also be used at the beach and the pool in the summertime.

Boots for cold or wet weather should be bought with care. You'll save money for getting the best quality, paying strict attention to the grade of rubber and leather. You'll have to pay well for the finest quality, but it should survive a whole winter, and still be available for a rainy summer day, too.

Rubbers are a question mark in my mind. My children never wear them, and will lose one before the first day is out. You have to know your own children to make that decision. For me, no rubbers.

As your children grow older and approach or enter their teens, you can still purchase undies, nightwear and such, sticking to your theories of prudence and hoping that your taste will be acceptable to the beneficiaries of all of this planning and attention. It is necessary to remember that individual tastes and preferences are developing at this stage, and sometimes they come on strong.

The absolutely beautiful navy blue classic dress that you buy on sale at Altman's for Nancy can remain in her closet for two years, a memorial to practicality, and commemorative of the fact that ever–changing teenage taste was not recognized or consulted.

Teenagers, being faddists, must buy the things that put them in the 'in' group. It's cruel to deny them these items if they can be bought cheaply, particularly if the teenager is willing to buy all or most of these items from his or her own allowance and earnings.

Needed, always, is mother's thoughtful guidance

when it comes to the remainder of the teenage outfit. Again the basics must be comfortable, durable and acceptable, and that usually means money. It has to be spent wisely."

11. The High Cost of Nesting

Students of family finance have often pondered the remarkable compulsion that drives people to over-spend in overfurnishing their homes. Even during the Great Depression, reduced–income Americans continued to provide better–than–average business for the suppliers of home furnishings and the many entrepreneurs and gadgeteers of the era.

The answer lies deep in psychology, of course, and has to do with the nest–building instinct that provides strong motivations for all humans. It's why little girls play house. It's why little boys build huts. It's why younger children will snuggle in little nests beneath chairs or behind the living room sofa.

It's an instinct that never dulls, but, in fact, intensifies as the years go on. It is not essentially related to mating, for even the owners of "bachelor pads" spend lustily to make celibate nests as snug and inviting as possible. With mating, however, the instinct not only intensifies, it is, of course, doubled and supplied from two sources—a twin motivation aimed at one shared pocketbook.

It is quite likely that motivational research would disclose that many of the men who buy cabin cruisers or cruising–size sailing vessels or build hunting or fishing shacks in the woods are frustrated in their nest–building instincts by wives who dominate in the furnishing of the home. It's not uncommon to hear a wife refer to it quite accurately as "my home," rather than "our home." It becomes a sort of familiar hotel to the breadwinner, a spot where he can pause and recharge his batteries, but where he never really owns anything in the way of furnishings; they're his wife's.

The basic guide for furnishing a home has two rules:

1. Shop with extreme care and due thought; don't buy by impulse.

2. Durability is more essential than style.

When it comes to home furnishings, durability and quality are not always related, but to a surprising degree, the higher the price and better the grade, the more mileage you'll get from almost any item of home furniture or furnishings. There are some wild exceptions, of course, and we'll mention some of them in this text.

It is more costly to furnish a home on a piecemeal basis, item by item, step by step, than it is to have sufficient money or credit to do a good share of the necessary buying all at once.

One of the principal reasons for this is that furniture bought on a piecemeal plan may have to be discarded later on when you get around to establishing a theme or motif in your home. Even the girls in junior high school these days know that in any one room you can't mix rock maple with mahogany or cherry antiques with walnut, or any of those with tubular chrome or Danish modern.

But a home, like a good marriage, has to evolve. Like a good marriage, it isn't made in heaven; it's made by hard work and much cooperation, understanding and patience. Thus it's not advisable to start out with some hard–and–fast motif in mind, unless you know exactly what the future holds and where you will make your *ultimate* home—the one you're likely to spend several years living in. This, in these days of high mobility, is not likely to be possible.

The young man who begins a career with a nation-wide corporation in Southern California may have a wife who is tempted to furnish her Mediterranean-style home in Spanish–accented furniture and furnish-ings. She may be out of luck when, two years later, he is transferred to Philadelphia and the home they buy right on the Main Line is adorned with oak–paneled walls and a fireplace with a mahogany mantle, and two years after that he is promoted to the New York office and they find they can afford to live in "New York's richest suburb," Fairfield County, Connecticut, where even swimming pool cabanas are made to look colonial and rock maple is required furniture even in doll houses.

The moral is that it's best to start with basics that are flexible and adaptable and that, in time and if neces-sary, can be "antiqued" or refinished to serve durably in almost any surroundings.

Young folks usually start with an apartment, and the chore of furnishing it generally is a budget–blasting experience. Marriage counsellors report that this expe-rience causes the greatest number of early marriage quarrels and is a far greater cause than sexual adjust-ment in sending a wife home to mother weeping over the cruel fate that has put her into the arms of an ogre.

Said ogre, meanwhile, may wonder why on earth he ever thought marriage would be fun, and he recalls, wistfully, the fine and comfortable bachelor quarters he vacated in order to espouse himself to a compulsive interior decorator.

The happiest time of life—furnishing the nest together—often becomes the most trying time of a new marriage.

So let's start by removing some of the strain for both husband and wife in the assignment of furnishing that first apartment.

1. You don't have to worry about style or motif. Buy what looks best with the apartment you're furnishing and forget about the future homes you may live in. It is accepted practice today, even in the rock maple country of Fairfield County, to mix the themes in a well–furnished home. You can have a colonial maple dining room and a Danish modern living room with Italian Provincial bedrooms and a Hong Kong rattan playroom. You can't mix them all together in one room, of course, but you can be in good style with a different motif in each room.

2. Save as much money beforehand as possible. If you can furnish your first apartment without going too deeply in debt, you're way ahead of the pack. If you think you're going to buy more than you have cash to pay for, be sure to establish your credit beforehand, rather than at the time of purchase. If your furniture–furnishings dealer handles his own credit (usually through his bank or a consumer finance company), sign all the papers and establish a "line of credit" at least a week before you do your actual shopping. This can be in units of $500 (that is, $500, $1,000, $1,500) and it's a reserve against which you can draw when you exhaust your actual cash. If your credit is cleared, and okayed,

use it prudently. Because it's such a painless way to buy things, credit is often abused.

3. Start with the bedroom—or master bedroom if there's more than one sleeping room. This is an important room; it's where pride in the nest–building starts.

4. It's not required that the first bedroom you furnish be something they'll want to photograph for *Better Homes and Gardens.* Settle for the practical. What you buy for your first bedroom can be used to furnish your guest room, should you move to larger quarters one day. A canopied bed is nice, you may have decided as you leafed through the magazines. It is, but it's expensive and not really necessary. On the other hand, it may be exactly what you need for your morale, so balance one factor against the other. You *can* get a perfectly comfortable, long-lasting, good-looking outfit consisting of box springs, four legs and a detachable headboard, at a much lower cost. This may permit you to put a little more money into a dresser, with a good-quality mirror, and a chest of drawers. Ample shelf room is more important even than closet space. Look for depth in your drawers; don't get the shallow kind that will not even accommodate a pair of rolled men's socks.

5. Select living room furniture for livability as well as style. You may find it useful to think of a cold, bleak rainy day and to imagine how "homey" your furnishings will make the apartment. Some stark, ultramodern piece may look nice in the showroom, but it may not lend the atmosphere you seek for home–building. A nest, above all, should be the most comfortable place imaginable.

6. If you intend to have children, it is not advisable to buy the best–grade rug or carpeting. It is also impractical to get the cheapest, for it doesn't survive even adult wear and tear. Find something with an in–between

price that does not show stains, cleans easily, and promises to provide some durability.

7. It is advisable, however, to buy the highest–quality appliances that you can afford, if you must provide some for your apartment kitchen. When it comes to stoves, ovens, washers, dryers, dishwashers, garbage disposals, refrigerators and freezers, there are certain self–protecting rules you must observe. First, beware of model changes. Make sure it's this year's and not last year's. You check this by consulting your women's magazines. If necessary copy down the model number and call the distributor listed in the yellow pages, and ask him point blank about the vintage of the machine bearing that number. Make certain that there is a guarantee or warranty and read it carefully. Be sure that the equipment can be serviced by a representative of the manufacturer—a low–priced machine with a strange–sounding name may have to be junked because a 30–cent part breaks and there's no one to fix it. If you buy equipment with odd features, such as a left–hand door, make certain it is a well–known brand with a fine service warranty so that it can be sold to those who may follow you in your apartment. You probably won't want to move it with you, but you may have to, if it's an oddball with an unknown name.

8. Don't, above all, overlook or ignore used furniture. Many times it is better to have a used article of superior quality than a similar piece that is brand new but cheap and poorly constructed. Offhand, you can't buy a better piece of furniture than those solid oak dining room tables that were made in the 1920s, which, a few years ago, you couldn't give away, because they were out of style. Look for quality, for durability, for strength. Those are the keys to good furniture.

9. Think about antiques. Don't plunge into the hobby without lengthy and learned exploration. More people

are gypped than satisfied in the antique market, and more lose money than make money when trading in them. Those who profit really know their stuff. However, any genuine antique item that you can buy to fill a specific need, is, on the face of it, a good buy. It will increase in value as the years go on, while almost everything else you own will depreciate. Be practical about it, though. Unless you want to make a hobby out of it, many antiques are highly impractical. You don't want a genuine whale oil lamp with cut-glass spangles and a Sandwich frosted glass globe, unless you know where there's a school of whales nearby ready to yield some blubber that can be boiled down into oil. If such an item attracts you as a desirable doodad, then remember: if children are expected in a family, all perishables must be of low value and easily replaced, for perish they will, no matter what precautions are taken. You don't want to inhibit a child because of a whale oil lamp, now, do you? Just remember, antique furniture isn't antique unless it predates the band saw. That was invented in 1846. If any article made of wood has regular sawyer's markings on it, you can be sure it was made after 1846. This is cited, not because the writer is even slightly knowledgeable about antiques, but merely to show you how easily you can be tricked. Remember, con men aren't confined to used–car lots and carnivals.

10. If you're hobbyless, think about developing one that will save you much money: furniture restoration, veneering and upholstering.

With such a hobby, you'll look at used furniture in a new light, seeing it not the way it is, but the way it can become. One very wealthy friend of mine has completely furnished his large mansion with magnificent furniture, every piece of which was bought secondhand and restored in his hobby shop in the basement. He and his wife share this form of relaxation. Neither one really has to be inordinately thrifty; it's a hobby they developed back in the lean years and they have come to enjoy it so much that it remains with them now, even though they could furnish a dozen homes without feeling the money pinch.

11. With children in a home, all furniture becomes a compromise. It is foolish to buy and use good-quality furniture or furnishings until the children are old enough to practice concern for their shared possessions. Muddy feet can be tracked onto a very expensive rug without permanent damage. Those same feet walking home from school on a road that has been freshly tarred, can cause irreparable and costly damage to that same rug. When it comes to any items that can be damaged by children, large or small, be careful about the size of your investment until you're sure the age of destructiveness has been passed. Instead, put your money into the bank to fight inflation. You'd rather have good children than a good rug, wouldn't you? Okay, don't get the good rug right away, and settle for the good children. By the time the kids are bringing home their own dates, you can be proud of your furnishings. Meanwhile, relax and save money.

12. Don't think that you have to furnish a home before you move into it. As you progress up the economic scale or move from place to place, don't be stampeded into unnecessary spending. Once you have the necessities, you can survive for awhile with some sparsely furnished rooms. That way you'll have a much better idea of exactly what you want in the way of furniture and equipment, and you can shop much more wisely. Even Dorothy Draper would have difficulty decorating a house all at one time. She starts with basics and moves carefully, step by step. You have the basics; you can move the same way. Take your time.

If prudence is your watchword, as it should be, it won't cost as much as you think it will.

In general, the foregoing has been a guide for young marrieds setting up housekeeping for the first time in an apartment or small home, but the basic rules need only be transferred to a broader canvas to apply to anyone facing any stage in the development of a home.

The increased mobility of the American breadwinner, and hence of the American family, results in some added cost and hardship to those who must move, but it has caused some benefits in the secondhand market that redound to the savings of those left behind. Those who must pack up and leave commonly decide to shed some of the burden and either sell some of their belongings to secondhand shops—many of which operate for the benefit of charities—or run "tag sales" in which they put price tags on whatever they want to get rid of, and open their homes to the public.

Anyone who is rounding out the furnishings in his home is wise to keep an eye on these two sources of used materials.

In our home we have a giant–sized pine–paneled kitchen with one area that simply cries for one of those huge old–fashioned round kitchen tables. We tried to buy one from several manufacturers and, aside from being stunned by the price, were told we'd have to wait until the proper trees were cut and seasoned and sawed, a process that might require a couple of years, at least.

We began watching the secondhand shops in our area, and after a patient wait of about six months, a rather dilapidated round oaken table, apparently early Sears, Roebuck Vintage, showed up. It had marvelous wood, so thick, so heavy it promised to be difficult to work with.

I bought the monster for $30, brought it home in a borrowed station wagon, and in two weeks had completely rebuilt its big center pedestal, removed all old paint and stain, sanded it down, and restored it with colonial pine finish. We bought unfinished chairs of colonial design and finished them to match. On our outfit we saved at least $200, and I'll match it for quality, workmanship, strength, durability and beauty against anything turned out in the custom workshops today.

A substantial portion of my own hobby workshop was acquired at small cost at tag sales. In our particular area there is an odd mixture of airline captains and key IBM executives. One can hardly imagine a more mobile group. A family will "settle down" in its home for two or three years when suddenly the master of the house is notified he must move on to another big, challenging job somewhere else.

From the process of packing—something that is almost routine—derive those wondrous tag sales.

Poor old Pete Pilot, who has been developing a woodworking hobby over the last three years, decides that in his new job, flying from Los Angeles to Tokyo, he won't have time for such relaxation, so he puts price tags on all of his tools and equipment and runs a small classified ad for a tag sale on the following weekend.

Charley Computer, who has spent a half–dozen years perfecting his huge organic garden, knows that the apartment IBM has for him in Berlin, just off the Unter den Linden, has no room for gardening, so all of his gardening tools and equipment get tagged and sold.

I attend these affairs with my Sears catalog tucked under my arm. That way I have a rough idea of the value of the items, and, with a little inspection, can tell if I'm being offered a bargain.

In outfitting my own shop I picked up a fine electric drill, three-speed, for $10. At another such sale I bought every size of bit to fit it for a total of $3. Hammers, screwdrivers, wrenches, pliers, saws, T squares and such all came from tag sales. For my own organic garden I got an excellent composter-shredder (a machine that makes mulch out of grass and leaves and vines) at less than half the original price for such equipment.

Not all sections of the country have such active secondhand markets, but every part of the nation has some such market. With a little searching, you can cut the price of many items you want by deciding to be a second owner.

12. Become A Property Owner

"When shadows fall
"And birds whisper day is ending,
"My thoughts are ever wending,
"HOME."*

That's what it's all about—HOME, be you bachelor, spinster, husband, wife, father, mother, butcher, baker or cabinetmaker, your days of toil are spent for one primary reason: to provide a home. It may not be much, but it's home. As such, it's the most important place in your life. It may be the shrine where you house your wife and children, or it may be that familiar old hole in the wall where you hang your hat, kick off your shoes, drink beer from a bottle and watch television shows you'd be ashamed to admit you liked, but it's home. It's the end product of the drive for security, the second most powerful compulsion in human behavior.

*From "Home," by Peter Van Steedan, Harry and Jeff Clarkson, Marlo Music Corp., c. 1931, assigned 1943 to American Academy of Music, Inc. Used by permission.

If it *is* a hole in a wall and not a vine–covered cottage or a manse on the hill, you are, if you're normal, dreaming of a grander place to call home. If you rent, you're likely planning to stash away a certain sum regularly until you have the equivalent of the down payment for a home in savings. (This is calculated at roughly 25 per cent of the asking retail price of a home—though 30 per cent is a safer figure.)

Though you may intend always to rent, for one reason or another, you won't feel secure—really secure—until you have the cash necessary to buy a home.

The trouble is, you may never have enough money in escrow, for the price of homes mounts with each succeeding year. It will continue to do so, well into the 1990s, and perhaps beyond, if only because of the pressures of the population explosion of the 1940s, 50s, and early 60s.

The population pressures make themselves felt first in hospitals, then in schools, and last of all in homes.

So the question arises, in order to protect yourself against inflation, should you buy or should you rent?

Ideally, you should buy.

Even the rudimentary arithmetic is on your side, if you buy.

Let's say you fall in love with a $40,000 home. If it's brand new, a bank will very likely lend up to 80 per cent of its value on a mortgage, or $32,000. You'll have to arrange for $8,000 cash. If it's not new, the bank quite likely will try to lend only 60 per cent of its value, or $24,000, and you'll have to arrange for $16,000 cash. If it's new–old, say, used a couple of years or so, you may be able to effect a compromise and arrange for a mortgage of about 70 per cent.

Local banks will do the best for you, usually, but they have hard–nosed notions about how much they'll lend on any specific house.

Banks are like City Hall—you can't fight 'em. Learn to adjust gracefully.

When you measure outgo on a home-with-mortgage versus outgo for rent only, it appears on the surface that the renter has the financial edge. It requires a different perspective for the proper evaluation of a home owned jointly by you and your bank.

Let's say that you buy that $40,000 home and that you have to put up 25 per cent in cash, or $10,000. Your mortgage of $30,000 at, say, 8 per cent interest, will require regular payments for the next twenty years.

Somewhere along the line you're going to stop short and say, "Why, heck, if I had left my $10,000 in the stock market, I'd be earning at least 8 per cent in dividends, plus, perhaps, some appreciation in capital. Even if I had left it in a savings bank, I'd be earning at least 5 per cent in interest or more."

True, true, but you'd be paying rent to a stranger. The rent you'd be paying would have no value except for the month that it provided shelter.

When you own your own home, jointly with a bank, the money you pay in mortgage amortization is paid to you. With each passing month your equity in the home increases—imperceptibly at first, of course, as heavy interest charges weight the monthly payments—but at a greatly accelerated pace as years go by.

In addition, the value of homes increases with each passing year in times of inflation, as much as 10 per cent or more in many parts of the country. This increase—regard it as a dividend—applies not only to the share you own outright, but to that portion owned by the bank, except that the increase is credited to you and not to the bank.

If in a year after buying it your home is worth $44,000, the bank still has claim to less than $30,000 worth of that value.

The $10,000 that you put in is now worth $14,000.

So you paid 8 per cent interest on $30,000, and you lost the 5 per cent or more you could have earned on your $10,000. This makes you come out about even, insofar as the arithmetic is concerned.

But the balance that you paid in amortizing your mortgage—say it's only $1,000 the first year—has increased your equity in the house by the same amount. That makes your total equity something in the neighborhood of $15,000.

Quite simply, you have put up $10,000 that in one year has increased in value by 50 per cent, *thanks* to inflation.

Question: can you match that with any other kind of investment?

So, in times of inflation, the advice is to buy property.

But what kind of property, and where?

First, look out for immediate needs. Look for a home. The best place is in suburban America, which, by all marketing standards, is just about everywhere but in a central city. Many volumes have been written about the best way to buy a home. There are simple caveats, however, that can be listed briefly.

· Pick the town and locality first, before you begin to look for the home or homesite.

· Check the town's master plan, or have your lawyer do it for you, to make certain plans are not under way for a superhighway through your future living room for a huge apartment complex across the street.

· Talk to someone about the tax situation. Does the community sorely need new schools, hospitals, sewers or other facilities requiring large expenditures of taxpayers' money?

· Check the accessibility of shopping facilities, schools, churches.

· Check on three basics: water supply, sewage disposal and the adjacency of fire hydrants. If you're out of a fire district, your insurance rates may be excessive, and total fire insurance is a *must*.

These are the few simple rules, and they're basic. Generally speaking, while buying a house can be a great investment, it can also be a terrible one if you're not sensible enough to make proper inquiry into the facts outlined in the foregoing.

The most beautiful home in the world, with a bargain price on it, may be situated in an area where a municipal sewer line will be installed within the next few years, calling for a special assessment outlay of several thousands of dollars from each abutting home owner. This must be calculated into the price of the house. And remember as well that municipalities don't give you time–payment schedules for paying your taxes, even for whopping special assessments. In almost any community near a big city, there are more non–home owners than there are property owners, so politicians allow for few special provisions for the chap owning his own home. They operate under an inflexible rule that calls for cash on the barrelhead. A fellow who can afford to own his home, they reason, can afford to pay his taxes. Generally, it's a safe assumption; but every home owner, on occasion, finds he's the exception who proves the rule.

There are compelling reasons, though, for searching out that dream home, checking it out for feasibility, and buying it, not only as a home, but as one of the primary havens against the forces of inflation.

It is not for me to tell you what kind of home to buy —Cape Cod, traditional, contemporary, or what have you. Your home must make *you* happy, and in some measure, it must reflect your personality.

Try not to buy more of a home than you think you'll need, but most of all, never buy less than you really need. Children, even of the same sex, will share a bed-room for only so many years. On the other hand, if this is the home from which you never plan to move, just remember that you can expect your children to move out sooner or later, leaving you with more room than you want to care for in your less vigorous years.

Like a boat, the ideal home, then, is a compromise. You seek middle ground between what you require at present and what you believe your requirements will be in the future. You seek to reach a rapport with your maximum and minimum housing needs.

For best investment possibilities, look for either a stable, well–settled community, or one with a great expansion potential. The latter can be tricky, though, for you may find yourself in the path of industrial or commercial development that might ultimately pay off, but would cause you some severe problems during the period of transition.

Waterfront property is always the best investment you can make, simply because there's a limited amount of it. Shorefront on an ocean or bay is highly desirable provided you don't locate a residential home in the midst of summer cottages. Similarly, lakefront and riverfront homes command respect from the real estate agents, banks and those who set prices.

Until man learns more about his environmental problems, though, beware of polluted waters.

The uninitiated may be unaware that the danger of pollution can be just as great on oceanfront property as along an industrial river. This is particularly so where mud or sand is building up, creating pools of stagnant water at low tide. You run the risk of discovering, a few years hence, that your oceanfront home is, in fact, separated from the ocean by several yards of impenetrable and noxious ooze.

On lakes, make certain to check on sewage disposal

facilities and whether cesspools are required for both year–round and summer or seasonal homes. On some lakes the residents or the communities continue to permit the unbelievable practice of installing sewage outfalls in the lake waters. Sooner or later this will be outlawed, requiring a substantial expenditure for cesspools or sewers, so the cost must be reckoned into the purchase price of the property or home.

The danger of pollution along industrial riverbanks is obvious. Throughout the world, however, environmental ecologists are winning their war against needless pollution of the earth's waters.

Only a few of us will be able to find choice waterfront sites, however, so the selection of a homesite will follow more conventional lines, though they are equally fraught with pitfalls. Three protective steps can keep you out of trouble: 1) careful scrutiny of the municipality's master plan; 2) employment of a good local lawyer; and 3) contact with a reputable, reliable local real estate agency.

What of the family, though, that wants to live in the central city or that believes it should live there for professional reasons? Or how about the fellow who simply hates to commute?

Some will be well heeled enough to buy their own apartment buildings or tenement buildings so they can live in one unit and collect rents on the others. In smaller cities this is not at all a bad device and is within the price range of many. It costs no more to buy a three–family tenement house in most cities than it does to buy a single–family home in the suburbs.

There's one difference, however: banks are a bit more agreeable in writing mortgages on such properties than they are on single–family dwellings, simply because of the rent–producing factor. A tenement owner who wants to live in one of his units and rent the remainder might be asked by a bank, under certain conditions, to assign a portion of his rents to paying off the mortgage. This is not at all a bad arrangement, for it means he'll be reducing his mortgage and increasing his equity in the property with the help of the other tenants. Essentially, it's easier than swinging the deal all by himself, as in the case of the owner of the single–family home in the country.

In the larger cities there are condominiums and cooperatives. The condominium, for most people, is the more practical, though, of course, it too embodies risks.

Under the condominium arrangement you make an outright purchase of your apartment. It is regarded as a separate entity and as such is salable or resalable. You pay your own taxes, and provide for your own upkeep, plus a small additional charge for your share of heat, light, air conditioning and elevator service. The point is, you own title to your own property, even though it may be suspended several floors above ground level in a nest of steel and concrete.

The one drawback with such an arrangement is that you do not have much control over your immediate neighborhood. You may keep your part of the building in A–one condition, but a couple of floors below, some fellow may be encountering rough financial problems and is letting his paint peel and plaster show wear. There's not much you can do about it. Most condominiums do have separate agreements among the purchasers, however, that provide for minimum upkeep under threat of penalty of some kind. Usually this takes the form of having the repairs paid for by the building committee and the cost, plus penalty charges, passed along to the delinquent. It's a small nuisance for such great value.

Cooperative apartment living is a bit more complex and usually more costly. It means essentially that you are buying an entire apartment building with a number of other families and sharing the cost, usually on a per–square–foot basis, with all of the others.

Of necessity, your down–payment is greater than it is with the purchase of a condominium. You also pay regularly to certain special funds for upkeep of the entire building and for the services provided to tenants. You may not be able to sell whenever you wish to, without permission from the other tenants.

Nevertheless, it, too, boils down to something better than merely paying rent to some landlord for an apartment that you lease for a certain period of time. The landlord has to make a profit on his investment, and, like it or not, you're contributing your share to that profit.

The central city dweller, no matter what arrangements he has for his apartment, would do well to set aside additional savings so he can buy his own place outside the city, even if he doesn't use it.

A sensible way to do this is to invest in a place you will use for vacations. Then, hopefully, you can rent it when you're not using it, thus getting others to share the cost with you.

A saver who is en route to becoming a financier and entrepreneur might, on the other hand, merely buy a home in the country for the purpose of renting it full time. It can become his little nest egg, working for him and preparing to hatch into a chicken–come–home–to–roost when he's ready to retire and leave the city.

No matter how it's handled, the ownership of property is an essential early step in the effort to combat inflation. Real estate is one of the very best hedges against the erosion of money's value. As prices and costs go up, the value of real estate marches right along with them.

13. The Inflation—
Fighting Stocks

By now it is almost axiomatic that the stock market, particularly common stocks, provides a convenient hedge against the ravages of inflation. Generally speaking, this is true. The broad–based averages show that stock prices rise faster than other prices pushed up by inflation.

If you owned a tidy number of shares in each corporation whose issues are traded on the New York Stock Exchange, you would, indeed, lick the forces of inflation. Since there are nearly 1,300 such issues on the New York Stock Exchange alone, it's not likely that you can take a strong position in all of them. If so, you don't need the counsel in this book, for you can afford to hire the best inflation–slayers in the business.

The trick for those of us with modest means is to find the common stocks that best protect us against inflation. Out of the welter of shares traded each day, which ones should we select?

First, let's step back a bit and look at the situation.

Why common stocks? Why not savings accounts? Why not, in fact, those ultrasecure U.S. savings bonds?

It takes but a few paragraphs to make the startling comparison of common stocks with U.S. savings bonds, and it's not very pretty.

Let's pick the ten-year period from 1958 to 1968—years of postwar conditions, cold war struggles and the emergence of the Vietnam war.

Suppose in January 1958 you bought a $100 U.S. savings bond, paying $75 for it. In January 1968 you could have cashed it in for $100, which, on the surface, represented a gain of $25.

In that 10–year period, the cost of living rose 17 per cent, meaning that in 1968, $100 bought in goods and services only what about $85 bought in 1958. The *real* gain, then, was only about $10, or $1 a year.

But that isn't all. You would have to pay income tax at the highest rate on the $25 "gain." In the lowest bracket this would amount to $5, meaning that instead of a $10 real gain over a 10–year period, it was really a $5 gain over the same period—a profit to you of 50 cents per year. In the topmost brackets this could bring about a net loss after payment of taxes. Remember that, the next time you hear of some rich person buying heavily in U.S. savings bonds. He may be actually taking a loss to support government bonds.

In the same period of time, from 1958 to 1968, the Standard & Poor's index of 500 stocks advanced by about 140 per cent. The prices of those common stocks advanced more than eight times faster than the rising cost of living at 17 per cent.

Even after taxes, if you were in these common stocks, you would have earned an average annual income of about 5 per cent of your original investment *exclusive of dividends.*

Had you invested some of your money in fast–moving

growth stocks or in some of the many special situations that cropped up during that ten-year period, you would have fared much better. And don't forget that there was a strong bear market in 1966, when many prices tumbled.

When a cub reporter on the financial beat asked Bernard M. Baruch his formula for successful investing that had yielded him millions, the wily old senior statesman got off a joke. It eluded the youngster and he dutifully copied it down and brought it back to his editor.

Baruch's formula?

"Buy 'em when they're low and sell 'em when they're high," the financier advised the cub.

That sums up with extreme neatness the whole formula for success in Wall Street. It omits, however, the two essential ingredients: How to tell when they're "low," and how to pick the low ones that will later become "high." You may add a third element: How to judge when a stock is at its peak, so you won't sell it before it reaches its high, or hold it after it has peaked and is on the way down again.

Judgment in these areas requires expertise of a high order. Mr. Baruch may have made a joke simply because the whole matter is so complex it not only defies capsule descriptions, but also requires years of experience to understand.

That's why the selection of a good broker is essential in any consideration of the stock market. A licensed broker, affiliated with a firm that is a member of the New York Stock Exchange, may be regarded as qualified to carry out your wishes in selecting inflation-offsetting stocks and in advising you when to "switch," that is, to sell one company's shares and buy another's.

Commissions are all the same, no matter what firm you deal with, so unless you have special personal reasons, it's wisest to deal with the most reputable broker-age house you can find.

Statistical studies have shown repeatedly that care-fully selected portfolios of the common stocks of lead-ing corporations, including many so–called blue chips, have proved to be considerably superior to gold as infla-tion hedges. For that reason, we do not recommend investments in gold, either in futures contracts or in bullion or coins, for your hedging operations.

It has already been pointed out that real estate, in-cluding good commercial rentable property, is one of the finest hedges against inflation. Consider, then, com-panies that operate at a profit, show a good growth potential, are well managed, *and are rich in real estate holdings.* Surely these would seem to offer one of the finest hedges possible against the losses of inflation.

A continuing real estate boom throughout the next decade of the seventies seems highly probable. Land holdings in or near fast–growing sections of the coun-try are perfect inflation hedges, and the companies owning such realty holdings should be attractive to in-flation–wary investors.

Quite often you'll find that real estate is purposely undervalued on a company's balance sheet and thus is not fully calculated in the going price of its stock. It is not uncommon, also, for companies on occasion to dis-tribute some land holdings to stockholders as a special dividend or spin–off. Aside from temporary tax prob-lems such a windfall might provide for the investor, it is an excellent hedge against inflation.

Your broker should be able to provide you with a list of at least fifty companies that have major real estate holdings.

These range from outright land companies (All–State Properties) to community developers (General Devel-opment) to newsprint companies (Great Northern) to utilities (International Telephone and Telegraph) to railroads (Northern Pacific) to pipelines (Panhandle) to film companies (Warner Brothers–Seven Arts) to lumber companies (Weyerhaeuser).

A company that owns land doesn't automatically qualify as an inflationary hedge, however. It must be able to forge ahead on its own, without counting on its assets in real property. It must have a product or service that seems likely to stand up well in the inflationary period ahead. It must be well managed. It must be well capitalized. These are qualifications you must discuss with your broker in settling on the stock you want for your protection.

Among other things to discuss with your broker is whether or not he believes we are facing a period of creeping inflation or runaway galloping inflation. Some stocks that are the best in times of runaway inflation are not the best for you in times of creeping inflation. Once your portfolio is set up, there is no harm in switching wisely. The most dangerous thing you can do is to remain "married" to a stock, unless, of course, you have special reasons.

There are other kinds of stocks that are valuable for hedging, depending on the type of inflation you expect to encounter, and they have little to do with real estate holdings.

These include, for instance, companies dealing in money, like banks and finance companies. They deal in a commodity that is in short supply during periods of galloping inflation and they can command greater profits for their services. Thus their stocks improve in value.

Consider also companies producing or selling necessities like food, tobacco, cotton, drugs, salt. These people can effectively raise their prices to match costs that mount when inflation gets out of hand.

Those corporations dealing in the production, extraction or sales of essential raw materials also require your attention when thinking of securities to provide you with a hedge. Such producers range the gamut from aluminum to copper to coal to natural gas to oil to lumber to sulphur to pulp to uranium.

Think also of companies with low labor costs, which are likely to remain low; of investment companies with high leverage; of some stocks with high leverage; and in some special circumstances, of the high–risk, high–income companies.

A word here about "leverage." This investment implies the use of a small financial lever to move a much larger amount of money or profit. Conventionally, moving money or profit involves corporate investment in highest-grade bonds or preferred stock, giving the company an investment portfolio not unlike that of a mutual savings bank governed by strict regulations and operating under the prudent-man rule; or the use of borrowed funds to retain corporate investment portfolios intact; or the issuance of rights, warrants, convertibility options, and such, to acquire or sell securities for the purpose of increasing profits.

If this is a bit unclear, think of it this way. A company that has raised its capital with preferred stock, bonds or some other form of borrowed funds, has perforce kept the ownership of common stock—the *real* ownership of the company—within narrower ranges than might otherwise have been the case.

It has a prior claim on its earnings. It must pay interest on its bonds and dividends on its preferred stock. But the prior claim is in a fixed amount and, if handled properly, relatively small. This cost does not go up when earnings increase. Quite simply, any increase in earnings above the level of the fixed amounts of prior claim has a direct and multiplied effect on the remaining common stock. What is left over in earnings for applied value to the common stock is greater than would be the case if high leverage techniques had not been employed and there was more common stock in existence.

Let's take two companies, ABC Corporation and XYZ Company. Each is capitalized at $10 million. ABC Corporation is capitalized with a debt load. It has $5 million in bonds and $2.5 million in preferred stock, both of which take precedence over the common stock, currently worth $2.5 million in the stock market. XYZ Company is as clean as a whistle and absolutely debt-free; its $10 million is all in common stock. Any increase in ABC Corporation's earnings will, after paying the fixed charges on its debt, be applied to only $2.5 million worth of common stock. Any earnings for XYZ Company will be spread over $10 million worth of common stock. And just remember, too, that any interest paid is fully deductible before taxes.

Thus, ABC Corporation has leverage; XYZ Company does not. XYZ may be a perfectly good investment, but as an inflationary hedge, ABC Corporation is far superior. Its leverage makes it so.

If you have been thrifty enough and have squirreled away a handy amount of investable funds, and if your income is in a sufficiently high bracket to cause you tax worries, you should also give consideration to the tax–exempt municipal bonds.

The federal government cannot impose a tax on lesser taxing entities, nor on the yield from financing lesser tax entities. Thus when municipalities issue bonds to raise money for schools, hospitals, sewers, water works, streets, fire departments, and such, the purchasers of those bonds say they're buying "tax–exempts," simply because the money paid to them in interest cannot be taxed by the federal government.

If you are in the $24,000-to-$28,000 taxable income bracket for a joint return, you can buy a high–grade 6 per cent tax–exempt municipal bond that has the equivalent value to you of 9.38 per cent.

Since the 6 per cent is not taxable, you would have to have an investment yielding 9.38 per cent in taxable income to yield the same net 6 per cent.

If your income goes higher, your equivalent yield goes up. In the $44,000-to-$52,000 range you would have to earn 12 per cent taxable yield to equal the 6 per cent tax-exempt money you receive from municipals.

As a class, only securities of the federal government have a better record for safety than do the municipals, though be sure you check your rating before you plunge. Some of the older Eastern cities have had trouble in the past, and may face it in the future. Some do not have wise taxing programs.

Earlier in this chapter we mentioned gold and gold stocks as candidates for hedging and said we didn't recommend them. Gold-mining stocks are tricky and balky things. They offer uncertain holdings. Usually they increase in value only when devaluation of the American dollar is expected or threatened or rumored. They are "trouble" stocks, and unless you are a sophisticated investor, well versed in the intricacies of the world monetary system and such sideline things as the gold futures market and foreign exchange and arbitrage of goods, then it seems wiser to hedge with the tools at hand that are easier to learn how to use.

This is not to say that some gold-mining shares are not good hedges. They are. But they're not for me—I'm too inexpert. I've lost money on them in the past and fear I would continue to do so in the future. Gold is a separate specialty, standing all by itself.

Contrary to widespread belief, ownership of gold coins, either of U.S. or foreign mint, is not illegal, provided the coins are retained in the United States and not transported abroad. They may be held both as a hedge against inflation and as a perfect hedge against devaluation. The supply is limited, so the demand is strong.

And this, too, is tricky. A $20 U.S. "Double Eagle" has gold content worth about $34 at the pegged official price of $35 an ounce, so it sells for well over $50 in the open market. How much should you pay for it to be protected? I don't know. Only a numismatic expert can tell you.

14. The Most Practical Car For You

For a great many years a car was a highly practical possession. Its cost of purchase has always been high in relation to average income, but never so high as to be priced out of the market.

In earlier days roads and highways may not have been so smoothly paved, but assuredly they were less clogged. Mechanical repairs of your car may have been required more frequently, but they were markedly less expensive by every monetary measure, and they were easier to get. Upkeep was easy. Of equal importance was the fact that cars didn't age so rapidly. The "built–in obsolescence" that exists in both style and parts to-day, hadn't been added to the auto industry's planning boards in the good old days. When parts wore out, they were replaced from well–stocked inventories. And when you drove your six–year–old Hupp downtown to the local movie house, you weren't made to feel like a bum by the kid who pumped gas into it and by the parking-lot attendant who placed it in a neat line next to the Graham–Paige and the Studebaker.

All of that has ended now, and ended, too, is much of the practicability of the automobile. As soon as the car became a necessity and an integral part of the family budget, it ceased to be a practical possession. What with planned obsolescence, radical style changes and a noticeable loss in durability, the motor vehicle of today has about the same degree of prudent practicality as, say, a dress cut to extreme fashion. It will be outmoded before it is worn out. Add to that the fact that many of today's cars manage to be worn out by the time they become outmoded—which is altogether too soon after purchase for most people.

Yet a motor car is, for most people, a necessity.

Which car to buy is the omnipresent question hovering over most breadwinners and the subject, by and large, is the most common one discussed at bars, barbershops and 19th holes. A comment about the virtues of an auto has been known to set off a car-wide rhubarb on a commuter train.

Are foreign cars better buys than American cars?

"Yes," shout hundreds of thousands of satisfied users.

"No," scream equal numbers of American–car owners.

Careful analysis of their reasons for being satisfied boils down to the simple equation: the car of the satisfied owner is the one that best suits his needs and pocketbook.

Usually the fellow who drives a car with which he is dissatisfied is a chap who has not done his homework. He has not considered why he needs a car, what useful functions it must perform for him, and how he can fit it into his family budget.

You have seen many instances of fellows who became "semismart" about cars only to develop poor judgment when it came to making the actual purchase.

"It is ridiculous," this fellow says, "to buy a large and heavy American car for my wife to drive to the grocery store and beauty parlor. She makes only short trips around our neighborhood and so she can get along with a little foreign car. It's silly to have her drive that Cadillac to the drugstore for a tube of toothpaste and use up three gallons of high-test gas doing it. Instead, I'll get her a nifty little job that gives her 35 miles to the gallon."

Before he goes to look at a Volkswagen, however, he must teach his Cadillac–bred bride to use a hand shift since, if she attained legal driving age after 1937, she probably has no knowledge of the use of the foot clutch and the stick shift. (The American automotive industry has never explained satisfactorily why, if the automatic transmission is an advancement in design, it costs more to get a car with an old–fashioned clutch and hand shift.)

Inasmuch as our hero is a busy man, he sends his wife to driving school to learn the tricks of the stick shift. Cost: $75. That, no matter how you look at it, represents quite a lot of gas, right there.

Our hero returns one evening to find his bride zipping around the neighborhood in a fastback convertible, leaving rubber at intersections as she up–shifts to gain her position in an impromptu drag race with the minister's wife. She looks so gosh-darn cute that he decides right then and there that the drab–looking bug of Deutschland fame is not for his ultrasmart chick.

So he jogs to the bank next day, arranges for a larger loan than he had planned for, and orders her an XKE in smart British racing green, with genuine leather bucket seats and four disc brakes for her protection, realizing that now she really needs protection.

The cost, of course, parallels that of the Cadillac. The consumption of petrol per kilo at least parallels that of the Cadillac. The wife looks a great deal smarter when she roars off in a cloud of macadam to buy her tube of toothpaste, but friend breadwinner, after all his effort, is not one whit smarter. Poorer, perhaps, but not smarter.

The point here is that a great share of the blame for the high cost of automobile–owning rests with the buyers of cars and not with their manufacturers.

Prime example: Almost every September, with few exceptions, the manufacturers announce that prices on new models will be somewhat higher than on comparable models the preceding year. They put the blame on rising labor costs and material costs. This should mean that the value of used cars also rises. It doesn't. Why? Because the public doesn't place corresponding value on used cars.

If the gentleman who wanted a less expensive car for his wife had bought the Volkswagen, or a Renault, or a Toyota, or a Fiat, or a Saab, or a Ford Maverick, he might have accomplished his purpose. Or he might really have saved some money by getting a fifteen-year-old car—say a Plymouth—and buying a rebuilt (factory-new) motor from Sears, Roebuck, and four good tires, then having a set of new brakes installed and a transmission job done by Aamco. When finished, he would have spent less than half the cost of a small new car, and his wife would have had a sturdy American–built vehicle that would have lasted her at least a half–dozen years with a minimum of trouble.

There's always that bugaboo of "throwing good money after bad," however. As repair costs mount on aging cars, a fellow begins to feel the mounting expense; so, taking a look at soft used-car prices and feeble trade–in allowances, he decides the most prudent thing to do is to trade for a new car, the spiffier the model, the better, and t'hell with worrying about the little details, like finance charges.

We have Morganesque attitudes about our cars.

At one time, Mr. J. P. Morgan had the largest, most luxurious steam yacht on Long Island Sound. When asked by a reporter how much it cost to keep it afloat, Morgan replied that if you have to consider the cost of a yacht, you shouldn't own one.

It was sound advice, of course, but somehow the philosophy haş become distorted in its application to cars—primarily because they are now a necessity—and we tend to ignore their cost. We pretend that they're like Morgan's yacht and no one should bother with such trifling, though omnipresent details, as the cost of operation.

There can be no question about a completely rebuilt and totally safe fifteen–year–old Plymouth or Chevy or Ford being a superior vehicle and a superior "buy" to a current–model foreign car in the small–car field, if it's to serve as a "second car," but it's almost impossible to get Americans to accept that truth.

One reason for the reluctance to give older cars their proper consideration is the dearth of skilled mechanics needed to restore them to factory–fresh shape. In this regard there is a common delusion that the owner of a new car with a service warranty can get mechanical help whenever he takes his late–model car to the agency where he bought it. It's completely false. He can't get such assistance without wasting enormous amounts of time and involving himself in confusing red tape, the product of the mysterious protocol of the repair shop. The owner of the most costly and newest car finds that service is given with great reluctance whenever he shows up at the repair shop, and that it requires vast investments of his precious time.

I say this as a man who has owned brand new models of cars ranging the gamut from Plymouths to Cadillacs to Jaguars to Ford Mustangs. As this book was under preparation I was driving a fairly new Mustang 8 when suddenly it blew the gasket of an intake valve. I went to three Ford agencies to get this mysterious ailment treated. Only at the third did I learn roughly what the cause of the trouble was; there the repair-shop foreman told me I'd have to take it back to the place where I bought it—a considerable distance away—in order to get it repaired. He flatly refused to do it. He represented an authorized Ford agency.

Of what value, I ask, was my service warranty?

If you find a good and willing mechanic these days, prize him as you would a good doctor or dentist. He not only may help you with your second-car problems, but may make it possible to keep your new car operating smoothly so you can get to work on time.

Next to TV repairmen, mechanics are prone to be the biggest racketeers outside the organized mob. An honest mechanic, who is also skilled, is a citizen of great consequence, and a friend to be cultivated. He's your key to getting maximum efficiency from the use of your car or cars.

It will pay you to step back and take a long look at your own car needs and analyze them, so that you may make prudent purchases and then drive at peak efficiency.

If you're in a business where you put much mileage on your car, you have to think of durability as well as economy in driving. The lightest car is not always the easiest on mileage. Quite possibly you may find that the cheapest car to drive any distance is a Rolls Royce or a Cadillac or a Lincoln Continental. They'll yield eighteen to twenty miles per gallon on the open road.

In the case of the Cadillac or Continental, however, you take a whopping depreciation bite during the first two years of ownership. A brand new Rolls should not be considered by anyone fighting inflation. A used Rolls, say, five or six years old, is something else again. It may be a most prudent buy.

Quite likely, though, the heavy driver may do well to look one step down the line at the wide range of so-called middle-priced cars falling into a financial spectrum from, say, the Oldsmobile at one end to the heavy Plymouth or Ford or Impala at the other.

If you buy a big car because you take long vacation trips a couple of times a year, or put on much mileage for some other reason, think twice about owning such a vehicle, and think three times or more about renting one for those special trips. You don't have to own a big car all year just because you travel a thousand miles twice a year to go fishing. You don't have to rent a Hertz Ford, either, you know. There's a rental agency not far from you where you can get a Pontiac or a Chrysler for a day or a month at a price you may find you can handle.

If you commute to work by car, you may not need one of the larger models. In fact, you may want just about the smallest car you can find. On the other hand, perhaps you might like to compromise and get a middle-sized model so that you can take an occasional weekend trip without being too cramped.

The second car is where you may really economize, and before you settle on the midget model for your housewife–chauffeur, give serious consideration to a thoroughly rebuilt older car in the middle–price range. Just remember that these days you can get "life–of–the–car" guarantees on transmissions, mufflers and shock absorbers.

If a car hasn't been in a serious accident, and its frame hasn't been bent or damaged, the deciding factor may boil down to the condition of its body, which is something you can judge for yourself without professional help. After all, even the cost of a brand new motor isn't extreme if the car's body will hold up for a predictable time. The collective cost of such things as a battery, four tires, a transmission, four brakes, wheel alignment, and an ignition system may come to a lot less than you think, when you measure the total against the purchase price of even the smallest new car.

After all, it's something only you can decide.

But a car is a big expense. It's wrong to pay it without exploring all of the angles. The right car for you may be large, medium or small; domestic or foreign; new or used; fancy or plain.

The selection available is so vast that there's no need for you to drive any vehicle that isn't completely efficient for you.

15. Go Ahead—
Be Cheap

One of the most hideous scenes in this inflation–ridden world is the spectacle of a hard–pressed breadwinner dutifully adding a lusty tip for a bored and indifferent waiter in a restaurant where he may never again be a patron. He may have had to wait an interminable time for his martini; his meat may have been overdone; he may not have received the vegetables he ordered, and the after–dinner coffee may have tasted brackish; but, by golly, it was absolutely necessary to leave the prescribed bounty to the dour, personalityless automaton who reluctantly carted the viands from kitchen to table. The custom decrees a 15 per cent tip at luncheon and 20 per cent at dinner.

Thus the more the restaurateur robs you with his inflated prices, the more you have to pay his employees who wait on you. The owner wins two ways—he makes a higher profit from his food and drink, and because you tip a higher amount there than in gin mills, he doesn't have to pay his help so much.

Even though the American housewife today has the most magnificent kitchen in all of history where she can prepare meals, Americans and Canadians "eat out" more than any other people, anywhere in the world. It averages out to almost one meal per week per family of four, discounting the lunches eaten in restaurants by working men. It accounts for the existence of some of the finest restaurants in the world in the two North American countries. It also permits survival of some of the worst.

I have eaten in many restaurants where the food was so good and the service so efficient that I have happily added 20 per cent or more to the bill. In common with most, however, I have automatically added 20 per cent to a check in a place I couldn't wait to leave.

I cite this as an example not only because it's so glaring and so universal, but because it conveniently illustrates how all of us contribute to inflation without a whimper, and it shows yet one more place where we can exercise some prudence.

Don't deny yourself that once–a–week dinner on the town if you can afford it. But don't automatically calculate the cost at 20 per cent more than it really is. If it isn't worth 20 per cent more to you, don't pay it.

The whole segment of the economy embracing what the economists call "service industries" has gone hog–wild with price increases. From restaurants to laundromats to movie houses to Broadway shows, prices have gone out of sight. Poor people can no longer kill an evening of boredom by seeing a movie without planning for it in the budget. For a man and his wife to see a Broadway show in New York City, it costs at least $100, if you include a dinner before or after the theatre.

The cost of filling in leisure time has become almost outrageous. For that reason, don't deny yourself a new television set if you need it. It can prove to be one of your wisest investments, for the cost of providing entertainment via the boob tube is small compared with almost all other sources of fun.

If a TV set costs $400 (and prices range from less than $100 to more than $800 for fine color sets), merely figure that as the equivalent of four Broadway shows, or twenty meals in a restaurant for a couple, or maybe thirty-five or forty movies. If you figure your $400 set will last a half–dozen years and provide you with seven–night–a–week entertainment, whenever you wish, it's a sound investment, indeed.

Look for other less expensive forms of entertainment. Are you playing your best bridge—or have you even bothered to learn the game at all? Have you tried Scrabble lately? Books are more costly than they were, but you may have forgotten the sheer pleasure of reading (of course, if you're reading this, I'm like the preacher scolding his congregation about absentees). And let me remind you about radio. In almost every listening area in the country you can find an all–news station as well as an all–music station. The former may provide you with many invigorating thoughts that lead to stimulating conversations around the hearthside, and the latter can furnish you with soothing sound that permits you to read or play games or pursue a hobby.

You don't have to go broke seeking entertainment. One of the wealthiest men I know has a hobby that occupies his time every night in a week and a share of every weekend, and his investment is less than $100 a year. It's raising house plants. Sound sissified? This guy was a varsity tackle in college and played top–flight polo until age and arthritis caught up with him a couple of years ago. He lives on an estate in the country and still chops his own firewood—by hand.

A great many of us have come to regard entertainment—a necessary part of our lives—as an item of considerable expense. Entertainment may involve some *expense*, but it need not be *expensive.*All you need do is give it some thought.

I'll give you some examples of real–life inexpensive home–grown entertainment.

· A man and wife in Wilton, Connecticut, spend almost every night painting canvasses. Neither one knew anything about art two years ago. The lady has already sold one canvas.

· The wealthy man who raises house plants has had uncommon luck with his Boston ferns, and propagates them in a window of his dining room where the light is just right. He sold twenty-three young Boston fern plants last year at $1.50 apiece, helping to defray the modest costs of his hobby.

· A friend, Jerry Toon, took up wood carving, and after an investment of $11 in equipment and stock, developed a hobby that last year yielded him $88 in net profit.

· A lady in Torrence, California, delights in making hooked rugs. Her neighbors provide her with scraps of cloth and other material and she renders them into delightful patterns. As handmade hooked rugs, they command a good price in a Los Angeles department store. Her part–time hobby pays her about $1,300 a year.

· A kooky friend of mine, a bundle of nerves, faced a drinking problem. To keep his mind busy, and his tense fingers away from the bottle and glass, he spent a month in the back room of a jewelry shop learning watch repairing. Now it's his hobby. He does it in his spare time. Last year's earnings—nearly $3,000.

· Two men of my acquaintance are becoming increasingly expert at chess. Each has a board set up by his favorite chair near the TV set in his home. They play by telephone each Tuesday, Thursday and Sunday night. When one makes a move, he phones his opponent, who makes the necessary adjustment on his own board. Now and again, for tension–breaking, they do the same on a double–sized checkerboard. Checkers is a cutthroat game when kings are wild on a double–sized board.

· In the home of a banker friend of mine in Montclair, New Jersey, a game of Monopoly has been going on two or three nights a week for almost a year. Every time someone wins, he lends out money, at interest, to the defeated players, thus keeping the "economy" going in a supergame.

· Furniture restoration is the hobby of another friend. He hasn't broadened it into a money–producing sideline yet, but he is turning his own home into one of the most delightfully furnished and decorated residences in the area.

· Marge loves to use her spare time knitting and crocheting. One Christmas she knit beautiful sweaters for each male in the immediate family and crocheted matching sweaters for his wife.

Too often we think that leisure-time activities require huge outlays of cash. They needn't; not if you expend a little thought and tailor your activities to your own personality so that you can find some inexpensive fun around your own house.

Let the overcharging folks in the "service industries" overcharge someone else.

Why not go ahead and reach that big basic decision— BE CHEAP.

Being too cheap, as shown in preceding chapters, can be self–defeating. If you have a choice of handkerchiefs at a half–dozen different prices, the least expensive may not be worth purchasing. Somewhere there's a middle ground.

That middle ground is the area you can profitably seek at every level of expression and existence. Quite likely it will provide you with the best, most prudent purchases in everything ranging from safety pins to automobiles to houses and retirement homes. Just remember, you can have a whole lot more fun owning a fourteen–foot skiff than the Cunard people had owning the Queen Elizabeth.

School yourself to think middle–ground—it's your one defense against inflation. If you succeed, you should wind up with more savings than you would have otherwise.

Then, if you put those savings to good use, as suggested in earlier chapters, you'll be on your way to licking the evil, eroding devil in the nation's burgeoning economy.

There can be no hard–and–fast rule; there can be no definitive guide; there is no magic formula. You must develop your own individual style of inflation–fighting. The object is simple: Spend less; save more; use your savings wisely to counteract the losses incurred by rising prices.

While the object is simple, the techniques are not. To be a successful inflation–fighter, a family must keep inflation constantly in mind and tailor living habits accordingly.

It must become a way of life, as ingrained in a family as the spirit of Yankee thrift must have been in colonial days. Those early settlers spread a reputation for hard bargaining throughout the world. It must have been well earned, for it endured a couple of centuries.

It is necessary to remember that children and young people today find it harder to understand the value of money than ever before in history. Not only does the affluent society surround them with high-priced products, but figures, themselves, have become meaningless.

It's impossible to make Nancy understand that she

can't have three dollars tonight to go to the movies
when fifteen minutes before she watched a TV news
show and heard that the government is planning
to spend umpteen billion dollars on its next space mis-
sile.

It is difficult for the average home owner to understand what's happening—much less pass the information along to his children.

The "free public schools" in my community require
that I spend about $10 per week per child every week
during the school year, for lunches, books, supplies, and
odds and ends. Then there are extras, such as funds for
dances or ski trips or class trips to museums. We
figured it to be about $450 per student per year. Since
we have two students in the "free" schools, this is $900
per year—enough to finance the purchase of a new car
over a three–year period.

But try to explain this to Dave, age fifteen, when he
wonders why the family's rapidly degenerating second
car can't be replaced.

Perhaps we really need a return to the old values—to
the days of brass–toed shoes and durable corduroy
"whistle britches"—if only to give ourselves a constant
reminder of the need for thrift and more thrift, bargain–hunting and outright scrimping.

We must stop thinking of ourselves as one–car
families, then two–car families, then, progressively,
two-car-and-one-horse-and-home-in-the-suburbs   families.

To make a stand against inflation, you must stand fast
at some point. Pick the spot and hold it. Pay off all bills,
then hold it some more. And start saving.

Save as though your old age depended on it—for it
does!

There's an old chantey from colonial days, written by
that extremely productive composer called "Tradi-

tional," and it's worth memorizing these days, just as much as it was in those pre–Revolution days. It goes:

> Now, save up your pennies,
>   And pile up your rocks
> And you'll always have tabaccer
>   In your old tabaccer box.
>
> For every little bit
>   Added to whatcha got
> Makes just a little bit more!

That song contributed as much to America's success as did "Yankee Doodle," sung at the same time and composed by the same "Mr. Traditional." It's time to revive "Tabaccer Box."

16. You Can't Win the Game Without a Scorecard

From page 122 through page 162 you'll find a wide variety of ideas for cutting the cost of *your* living. They are intended more for inspiration than as guides. Methods that help us to fight inflation in our house, may not be desirable in yours; devices calculated to *use* inflation to *battle* inflation may work fine for everyone, but not all families will want to make every effort.

There is, however, one thing certain. If you want to do a capable job of beating inflation by using it, you have to know exactly where you're to make the effort. It will do you little good to cut back on the cost of clothing if it's food that is pushing up the cost of living. At best you'll add nothing to the savings account, and probably your reduction in clothing costs won't match the increase in food costs.

The only way to know where to apply the pressure in time to do any good is by keeping your own records. They may be informal, but if they're maintained,

they'll be informative. You can't rely on the government agencies to provide you with the information you
require. The Bureau of Labor Statistics does make
monthly and quarterly announcements about the cost
of living in the large metropolitan areas such as New
York, Chicago and Los Angeles, but the statistics lag by
ninety days. You will be notified in June that prices rose
in April. That's too late to help you in your calculated
battle against inflation.

And in case you live outside a major metropolitan
area, you may have to wait a full year to learn the vital
facts about costs in the region where you live. Remember, too, that regional statistics don't always apply to
the community where you do your shopping.

If average annual income for all Americans increases by, say, 5 per cent during the course of a year,
and your family shares in that increase, the only way
it can prove to be a benefit to you and result in an
increase in *real* income is by countering the inevitable
5 per cent rise in the cost of living. You can do that, no
matter where you live, only if you have some records to
guide you.

Keeping records is a drudge and a nuisance, and most
people can't even keep a family budget or maintain
their own tax accounts. The Internal Revenue Service
relies on the fact that a high percentage of middle-
income and lower-income Americans will use "ball-
park figures" in their tax returns, thus paying more
than they actually should on their taxes, simply because they haven't kept full records. This is not generally so with the rich, who usually are helped by experts
in the preparation of their returns, and must be mindful of the tax bite throughout the year.

The truth is, most people don't keep accurate records
because they figure—usually correctly—that the
amount of tax money they would save with precise

figures wouldn't justify all of the work involved in keeping score.

In fighting inflation, however, it is worth the effort.

If you're managing to save 5 percent of your annual income, or perhaps twice that, simply by keeping some weekly records, you'll be well paid for your time. If your income is $10,000 a year and you deflate your costs by 5 per cent of your income, you've saved $500, which is two-and-a-half weeks' pay.

The record-keeping needn't take more than a few minutes of your time, once a week—or even once a month, if you have a good memory.

The last twenty-four pages in this book are blank record sheets for keeping a full year's figures. You don't have to start with January, for inflation doesn't recognize a calendar year. Start at the beginning of next month.

On the record sheets you'll find listed both the broad categories of expenditures and some, such as food and clothing, in detail.

It may seem silly to differentiate between fresh vegetables and frozen vegetables, but if you'll watch prices during the changing seasons, you'll see that it isn't. The same holds true for packaged and processed foods.

With the figures down in black and white, you may observe for yourself that it's wiser to buy confectioner's sugar and baking chocolate for a few pennies and to make your own frosting for the cake you bake, than it is to spend many times that amount for a prepared frosting mix.

The record-keeping is self-explanatory. You won't fill every line each month, of course. But as the months pass by, you'll have an accurate idea of how you're spending your money.

Run a total each month, and make a comparison with the previous month. (You won't be able to do this the first month, unless you have an excellent memory.) As the months go by, you can spot immediately where you must shift gears, change your buying strategy, and begin to practice some old-fashioned thrift.

It turns out to be somewhat of a game, but it's a serious game, for it can cost you much money if you don't play it, and it can save you much, if you do.

Month of _____, 19_____

	1st Week	2nd Week	3rd Week	4th Week	5th Week*	This Month	Last Month
BASICS							
Rent or mortgage							
Fuel (heat)							
Light							
Phone							
Household repairs							
Appliance repairs							
Life insurance							
Other insurances							
FOOD							
Fresh meats							
Frozen meats							
Fresh vegetables							
Frozen vegetables							
Fresh fruits							
Frozen fruits							
Canned goods							
Packaged goods							
Processed foods							
Household items							
HEALTH & PROFESSIONAL							
Lawyer							
Doctor							
Dentist							
Optometrist							
Druggist							
Other							
FINANCIAL							
Auto loans							
Auto insurance							
Bank loans							
Other loans							
Educational costs							

(*) Where fifth week applies

Month of _____, 19____

	1st Week	2nd Week	3rd Week	4th Week	5th Week	This Month	Last Month
CLOTHING							
Men's haberdashery							
Men's suits							
Men's sports clothes							
Men's outerwear							
Women's underwear							
Dresses, skirts, blouses							
Women's sports clothes							
Women's outerwear							
Children's clothing							
Shoes							
HOUSEHOLD							
Appliances							
Furniture							
Furnishings							
Utensils							
Lawn & Grounds							
TAXES							
Withholding							
Social Security							
Federal (IRS)							
State (sales)							
State (direct)							
Real estate & local							
TRANSPORTATION							
Gas & oil							
Fares							
Car repairs, parts							
Tolls, parking							
MISCELLANEOUS							
Travel							
Entertainment & vacation							
Entertainment, others							
Unexpected							
Frivolous							

Month of _____, 19____

	1st Week	2nd Week	3rd Week	4th Week	5th Week*	This Month	Last Month
BASICS							
Rent or mortgage							
Fuel (heat)							
Light							
Phone							
Household repairs							
Appliance repairs							
Life insurance							
Other insurances							
FOOD							
Fresh meats							
Frozen meats							
Fresh vegetables							
Frozen vegetables							
Fresh fruits							
Frozen fruits							
Canned goods							
Packaged goods							
Processed foods							
Household items							
HEALTH & PROFESSIONAL							
Lawyer							
Doctor							
Dentist							
Optometrist							
Druggist							
Other							
FINANCIAL							
Auto loans							
Auto insurance							
Bank loans							
Other loans							
Educational costs							

(*) Where fifth week applies

Month of _____, 19____

	1st Week	2nd Week	3rd Week	4th Week	5th Week	This Month	Last Month
CLOTHING							
Men's haberdashery							
Men's suits							
Men's sports clothes							
Men's outerwear							
Women's underwear							
Dresses, skirts, blouses							
Women's sports clothes							
Women's outerwear							
Children's clothing							
Shoes							
HOUSEHOLD							
Appliances							
Furniture							
Furnishings							
Utensils							
Lawn & Grounds							
TAXES							
Withholding							
Social Security							
Federal (IRS)							
State (sales)							
State (direct)							
Real estate & local							
TRANSPORTATION							
Gas & oil							
Fares							
Car repairs, parts							
Tolls, parking							
MISCELLANEOUS							
Travel							
Entertainment & vacation							
Entertainment, others							
Unexpected							
Frivolous							

Month of _____, 19_____

	1st Week	2nd Week	3rd Week	4th Week	5th Week*	This Month	Last Month
BASICS							
Rent or mortgage							
Fuel (heat)							
Light							
Phone							
Household repairs							
Appliance repairs							
Life insurance							
Other insurances							
FOOD							
Fresh meats							
Frozen meats							
Fresh vegetables							
Frozen vegetables							
Fresh fruits							
Frozen fruits							
Canned goods							
Packaged goods							
Processed foods							
Household items							
HEALTH & PROFESSIONAL							
Lawyer							
Doctor							
Dentist							
Optometrist							
Druggist							
Other							
FINANCIAL							
Auto loans							
Auto insurance							
Bank loans							
Other loans							
Educational costs							

(*) Where fifth week applies

Month of _____, 19____

	1st Week	2nd Week	3rd Week	4th Week	5th Week	This Month	Last Month
CLOTHING							
Men's haberdashery							
Men's suits							
Men's sports clothes							
Men's outerwear							
Women's underwear							
Dresses, skirts, blouses							
Women's sports clothes							
Women's outerwear							
Children's clothing							
Shoes							
HOUSEHOLD							
Appliances							
Furniture							
Furnishings							
Utensils							
Lawn & Grounds							
TAXES							
Withholding							
Social Security							
Federal (IRS)							
State (sales)							
State (direct)							
Real estate & local							
TRANSPORTATION							
Gas & oil							
Fares							
Car repairs, parts							
Tolls, parking							
MISCELLANEOUS							
Travel							
Entertainment & vacation							
Entertainment, others							
Unexpected							
Frivolous							

Month of _____, 19_____

	1st Week	2nd Week	3rd Week	4th Week	5th Week*	This Month	Last Month
BASICS							
Rent or mortgage							
Fuel (heat)							
Light							
Phone							
Household repairs							
Appliance repairs							
Life insurance							
Other insurances							
FOOD							
Fresh meats							
Frozen meats							
Fresh vegetables							
Frozen vegetables							
Fresh fruits							
Frozen fruits							
Canned goods							
Packaged goods							
Processed foods							
Household items							
HEALTH & PROFESSIONAL							
Lawyer							
Doctor							
Dentist							
Optometrist							
Druggist							
Other							
FINANCIAL							
Auto loans							
Auto insurance							
Bank loans							
Other loans							
Educational costs							

(*) Where fifth week applies

Month of _____, 19____

	1st Week	2nd Week	3rd Week	4th Week	5th Week	This Month	Last Month
CLOTHING							
Men's haberdashery							
Men's suits							
Men's sports clothes							
Men's outerwear							
Women's underwear							
Dresses, skirts, blouses							
Women's sports clothes							
Women's outerwear							
Children's clothing							
Shoes							
HOUSEHOLD							
Appliances							
Furniture							
Furnishings							
Utensils							
Lawn & Grounds							
TAXES							
Withholding							
Social Security							
Federal (IRS)							
State (sales)							
State (direct)							
Real estate & local							
TRANSPORTATION							
Gas & oil							
Fares							
Car repairs, parts							
Tolls, parking							
MISCELLANEOUS							
Travel							
Entertainment & vacation							
Entertainment, others							
Unexpected							
Frivolous							

Month of _____, 19_____

	1st Week	2nd Week	3rd Week	4th Week	5th Week*	This Month	Last Month
BASICS Rent or mortgage							
Fuel (heat)							
Light							
Phone							
Household repairs							
Appliance repairs							
Life insurance							
Other insurances							
FOOD Fresh meats							
Frozen meats							
Fresh vegetables							
Frozen vegetables							
Fresh fruits							
Frozen fruits							
Canned goods							
Packaged goods							
Processed foods							
Household items							
HEALTH & PROFESSIONAL Lawyer							
Doctor							
Dentist							
Optometrist							
Druggist							
Other							
FINANCIAL Auto loans							
Auto insurance							
Bank loans							
Other loans							
Educational costs							

(*) Where fifth week applies

Month of _____, 19____

	1st Week	2nd Week	3rd Week	4th Week	5th Week	This Month	Last Month
CLOTHING							
Men's haberdashery							
Men's suits							
Men's sports clothes							
Men's outerwear							
Women's underwear							
Dresses, skirts, blouses							
Women's sports clothes							
Women's outerwear							
Children's clothing							
Shoes							
HOUSEHOLD							
Appliances							
Furniture							
Furnishings							
Utensils							
Lawn & Grounds							
TAXES							
Withholding							
Social Security							
Federal (IRS)							
State (sales)							
State (direct)							
Real estate & local							
TRANSPORTATION							
Gas & oil							
Fares							
Car repairs, parts							
Tolls, parking							
MISCELLANEOUS							
Travel							
Entertainment & vacation							
Entertainment, others							
Unexpected							
Frivolous							

Month of _____, 19____

	1st Week	2nd Week	3rd Week	4th Week	5th Week*	This Month	Last Month
BASICS							
Rent or mortgage							
Fuel (heat)							
Light							
Phone							
Household repairs							
Appliance repairs							
Life insurance							
Other insurances							
FOOD							
Fresh meats							
Frozen meats							
Fresh vegetables							
Frozen vegetables							
Fresh fruits							
Frozen fruits							
Canned goods							
Packaged goods							
Processed foods							
Household items							
HEALTH & PROFESSIONAL							
Lawyer							
Doctor							
Dentist							
Optometrist							
Druggist							
Other							
FINANCIAL							
Auto loans							
Auto insurance							
Bank loans							
Other loans							
Educational costs							

(*) Where fifth week applies

Month of _____, 19____

	1st Week	2nd Week	3rd Week	4th Week	5th Week	This Month	Last Month
CLOTHING							
Men's haberdashery							
Men's suits							
Men's sports clothes							
Men's outerwear							
Women's underwear							
Dresses, skirts, blouses							
Women's sports clothes							
Women's outerwear							
Children's clothing							
Shoes							
HOUSEHOLD							
Appliances							
Furniture							
Furnishings							
Utensils							
Lawn & Grounds							
TAXES							
Withholding							
Social Security							
Federal (IRS)							
State (sales)							
State (direct)							
Real estate & local							
TRANSPORTATION							
Gas & oil							
Fares							
Car repairs, parts							
Tolls, parking							
MISCELLANEOUS							
Travel							
Entertainment & vacation							
Entertainment, others							
Unexpected							
Frivolous							

Month of _____, 19____

	1st Week	2nd Week	3rd Week	4th Week	5th Week*	This Month	Last Month
BASICS							
Rent or mortgage							
Fuel (heat)							
Light							
Phone							
Household repairs							
Appliance repairs							
Life insurance							
Other insurances							
FOOD							
Fresh meats							
Frozen meats							
Fresh vegetables							
Frozen vegetables							
Fresh fruits							
Frozen fruits							
Canned goods							
Packaged goods							
Processed foods							
Household items							
HEALTH & PROFESSIONAL							
Lawyer							
Doctor							
Dentist							
Optometrist							
Druggist							
Other							
FINANCIAL							
Auto loans							
Auto insurance							
Bank loans							
Other loans							
Educational costs							

(*) Where fifth week applies

Month of _____, 19____

	1st Week	2nd Week	3rd Week	4th Week	5th Week	This Month	Last Month
CLOTHING							
Men's haberdashery							
Men's suits							
Men's sports clothes							
Men's outerwear							
Women's underwear							
Dresses, skirts, blouses							
Women's sports clothes							
Women's outerwear							
Children's clothing							
Shoes							
HOUSEHOLD							
Appliances							
Furniture							
Furnishings							
Utensils							
Lawn & Grounds							
TAXES							
Withholding							
Social Security							
Federal (IRS)							
State (sales)							
State (direct)							
Real estate & local							
TRANSPORTATION							
Gas & oil							
Fares							
Car repairs, parts							
Tolls, parking							
MISCELLANEOUS							
Travel							
Entertainment & vacation							
Entertainment, others							
Unexpected							
Frivolous							

Month of _____, 19_____

	1st Week	2nd Week	3rd Week	4th Week	5th Week*	This Month	Last Month
BASICS							
Rent or mortgage							
Fuel (heat)							
Light							
Phone							
Household repairs							
Appliance repairs							
Life insurance							
Other insurances							
FOOD							
Fresh meats							
Frozen meats							
Fresh vegetables							
Frozen vegetables							
Fresh fruits							
Frozen fruits							
Canned goods							
Packaged goods							
Processed foods							
Household items							
HEALTH & PROFESSIONAL							
Lawyer							
Doctor							
Dentist							
Optometrist							
Druggist							
Other							
FINANCIAL							
Auto loans							
Auto insurance							
Bank loans							
Other loans							
Educational costs							

(*) Where fifth week applies

Month of _____, 19_____

	1st Week	2nd Week	3rd Week	4th Week	5th Week	This Month	Last Month
CLOTHING Men's haberdashery							
Men's suits							
Men's sports clothes							
Men's outerwear							
Women's underwear							
Dresses, skirts, blouses							
Women's sports clothes							
Women's outerwear							
Children's clothing							
Shoes							
HOUSEHOLD Appliances							
Furniture							
Furnishings							
Utensils							
Lawn & Grounds							
TAXES Withholding							
Social Security							
Federal (IRS)							
State (sales)							
State (direct)							
Real estate & local							
TRANSPORTATION Gas & oil							
Fares							
Car repairs, parts							
Tolls, parking							
MISCELLANEOUS Travel							
Entertainment & vacation							
Entertainment, others							
Unexpected							
Frivolous							

Month of _____, 19_____

	1st Week	2nd Week	3rd Week	4th Week	5th Week*	This Month	Last Month
BASICS							
Rent or mortgage							
Fuel (heat)							
Light							
Phone							
Household repairs							
Appliance repairs							
Life insurance							
Other insurances							
FOOD							
Fresh meats							
Frozen meats							
Fresh vegetables							
Frozen vegetables							
Fresh fruits							
Frozen fruits							
Canned goods							
Packaged goods							
Processed foods							
Household items							
HEALTH & PROFESSIONAL							
Lawyer							
Doctor							
Dentist							
Optometrist							
Druggist							
Other							
FINANCIAL							
Auto loans							
Auto insurance							
Bank loans							
Other loans							
Educational costs							

(*) Where fifth week applies

Month of _____, 19_____

	1st Week	2nd Week	3rd Week	4th Week	5th Week	This Month	Last Month
CLOTHING							
Men's haberdashery							
Men's suits							
Men's sports clothes							
Men's outerwear							
Women's underwear							
Dresses, skirts, blouses							
Women's sports clothes							
Women's outerwear							
Children's clothing							
Shoes							
HOUSEHOLD							
Appliances							
Furniture							
Furnishings							
Utensils							
Lawn & Grounds							
TAXES							
Withholding							
Social Security							
Federal (IRS)							
State (sales)							
State (direct)							
Real estate & local							
TRANSPORTATION							
Gas & oil							
Fares							
Car repairs, parts							
Tolls, parking							
MISCELLANEOUS							
Travel							
Entertainment & vacation							
Entertainment, others							
Unexpected							
Frivolous							

Month of _____, 19_____

	1st Week	2nd Week	3rd Week	4th Week	5th Week*	This Month	Last Month
BASICS							
Rent or mortgage							
Fuel (heat)							
Light							
Phone							
Household repairs							
Appliance repairs							
Life insurance							
Other insurances							
FOOD							
Fresh meats							
Frozen meats							
Fresh vegetables							
Frozen vegetables							
Fresh fruits							
Frozen fruits							
Canned goods							
Packaged goods							
Processed foods							
Household items							
HEALTH & PROFESSIONAL							
Lawyer							
Doctor							
Dentist							
Optometrist							
Druggist							
Other							
FINANCIAL							
Auto loans							
Auto insurance							
Bank loans							
Other loans							
Educational costs							

(*) Where fifth week applies

Month of _____, 19_____

	1st Week	2nd Week	3rd Week	4th Week	5th Week	This Month	Last Month
CLOTHING							
Men's haberdashery							
Men's suits							
Men's sports clothes							
Men's outerwear							
Women's underwear							
Dresses, skirts, blouses							
Women's sports clothes							
Women's outerwear							
Children's clothing							
Shoes							
HOUSEHOLD							
Appliances							
Furniture							
Furnishings							
Utensils							
Lawn & Grounds							
TAXES							
Withholding							
Social Security							
Federal (IRS)							
State (sales)							
State (direct)							
Real estate & local							
TRANSPORTATION							
Gas & oil							
Fares							
Car repairs, parts							
Tolls, parking							
MISCELLANEOUS							
Travel							
Entertainment & vacation							
Entertainment, others							
Unexpected							
Frivolous							

Month of _____, 19_____

	1st Week	2nd Week	3rd Week	4th Week	5th Week*	This Month	Last Month
BASICS							
Rent or mortgage							
Fuel (heat)							
Light							
Phone							
Household repairs							
Appliance repairs							
Life insurance							
Other insurances							
FOOD							
Fresh meats							
Frozen meats							
Fresh vegetables							
Frozen vegetables							
Fresh fruits							
Frozen fruits							
Canned goods							
Packaged goods							
Processed foods							
Household items							
HEALTH & PROFESSIONAL							
Lawyer							
Doctor							
Dentist							
Optometrist							
Druggist							
Other							
FINANCIAL							
Auto loans							
Auto insurance							
Bank loans							
Other loans							
Educational costs							

(*) Where fifth week applies

Month of _____, 19____

	1st Week	2nd Week	3rd Week	4th Week	5th Week	This Month	Last Month
CLOTHING							
Men's haberdashery							
Men's suits							
Men's sports clothes							
Men's outerwear							
Women's underwear							
Dresses, skirts, blouses							
Women's sports clothes							
Women's outerwear							
Children's clothing							
Shoes							
HOUSEHOLD							
Appliances							
Furniture							
Furnishings							
Utensils							
Lawn & Grounds							
TAXES							
Withholding							
Social Security							
Federal (IRS)							
State (sales)							
State (direct)							
Real estate & local							
TRANSPORTATION							
Gas & oil							
Fares							
Car repairs, parts							
Tolls, parking							
MISCELLANEOUS							
Travel							
Entertainment & vacation							
Entertainment, others							
Unexpected							
Frivolous							

Month of _____, 19____

	1st Week	2nd Week	3rd Week	4th Week	5th Week*	This Month	Last Month
BASICS							
Rent or mortgage							
Fuel (heat)							
Light							
Phone							
Household repairs							
Appliance repairs							
Life insurance							
Other insurances							
FOOD							
Fresh meats							
Frozen meats							
Fresh vegetables							
Frozen vegetables							
Fresh fruits							
Frozen fruits							
Canned goods							
Packaged goods							
Processed foods							
Household items							
HEALTH & PROFESSIONAL							
Lawyer							
Doctor							
Dentist							
Optometrist							
Druggist							
Other							
FINANCIAL							
Auto loans							
Auto insurance							
Bank loans							
Other loans							
Educational costs							

(*) Where fifth week applies

Month of _____, 19_____

	1st Week	2nd Week	3rd Week	4th Week	5th Week	This Month	Last Month
CLOTHING							
Men's haberdashery							
Men's suits							
Men's sports clothes							
Men's outerwear							
Women's underwear							
Dresses, skirts, blouses							
Women's sports clothes							
Women's outerwear							
Children's clothing							
Shoes							
HOUSEHOLD							
Appliances							
Furniture							
Furnishings							
Utensils							
Lawn & Grounds							
TAXES							
Withholding							
Social Security							
Federal (IRS)							
State (sales)							
State (direct)							
Real estate & local							
TRANSPORTATION							
Gas & oil							
Fares							
Car repairs, parts							
Tolls, parking							
MISCELLANEOUS							
Travel							
Entertainment & vacation							
Entertainment, others							
Unexpected							
Frivolous							